Praise for
One of Us Must Be Crazy . . .

Conflict is common to all marriages. What MOST marriages don't have is a blueprint for resolving conflict when it occurs. Tim and Joy not only share with you THE most effective blueprint, but they will give you the practical tools and coaching needed in marriages today. Buy and apply this book! It'll revolutionize your relationship.

Dr. Dennis Rainey
President, FamilyLife

Conflict either makes love better or causes it to turn bitter. Tim and Joy Downs' book is a GPS for couples who want a safe and passable route through the maze of married couple conflict.

Dr. Tim Kimmel
Author of *Grace Based Parenting*

ONE OF US MUST BE CRAZY

...AND I'M PRETTY SURE IT'S YOU

Making Sense of the Differences That Divide Us

TIM & JOY DOWNS

MOODY PUBLISHERS

CHICAGO

All Scripture quotations, unless otherwise indicated, are taken from the *New American Standard Bible®*, Copyright © 1960, 1962, 1963, 1968, 1971, 1972, 1973, 1975, 1977, 1995 by The Lockman Foundation. Used by permission. (www.Lockman.org)

Scripture quotations marked NIV are taken from the Holy Bible, New International Version®, NIV®. Copyright © 1973, 1978, 1984 by Biblica, Inc.™ Used by permission of Zondervan. All rights reserved worldwide.

Scripture quotations marked NLT are taken from the Holy Bible, New Living Translation, copyright © 1996, 2004. Used by permission of Tyndale House Publishers, Inc., Wheaton, Illinois 60189, U.S.A. All rights reserved.

Scripture quotations marked THE MESSAGE are from The Message, copyright © by Eugene H. Peterson 1993, 1994, 1995. Used by permission of NavPress Publishing Group.

Published in association with the literary agency of Alive Communications, Inc., 7680 Goddard Street, Suite 200, Colorado Springs, Colorado 80920.

Edited by Cheryl Dunlop (2003) and Pam Pugh (2010)
Interior and cover design: Smartt Guys design

LIBRARY OF CONGRESS CATALOGING-IN-PUBLICATION DATA
Downs, Tim.
   One of us must be crazy—and I'm pretty sure it's you : making sense of the differences that divide us / Tim and Joy Downs.
      p. cm.
   Includes bibliographical references.
   ISBN 978-0-8024-1427-4
   1. Individual differences. 2. Marriage. 3. Conflict management. 4. Marriage--Religious aspects—Christianity. I. Downs, Joy. II. Title.
   BF697.D69 2010
   646.7'8--dc22

                          2010005061

We hope you enjoy this book from Moody Publishers. Our goal is to provide high-quality, thought-provoking books and products that connect truth to your real needs and challenges. For more information on other books and products written and produced from a biblical perspective, go to www.moodypublishers.com or write to:

Moody Publishers
820 N. LaSalle Boulevard
Chicago, IL 60610

1 3 5 7 9 10 8 6 4 2

Printed in the United States of America

For Joy's parents, Bill and Laura Burns
Thank you for demonstrating a love for God,
for each other, and for your family for more than half a century.
Thank you for being a model to us
in your commitment to cling to each other
through happy and difficult times.
You have made our lives more secure and joyful,
and we love and respect you both.

To our precious children, Tommy, Erin, and Kelsey
Though we do not know who your mates will be,
we pray that God will give each of you
a husband or wife devoted to Him and to you.
It is our prayer that each of you will strive to please God
and stay committed to your mate
as you learn how to love your partner for better and for worse.
We love you more than we can ever say.

CONTENTS

"You don't have to be sarcastic. All I said was,
'I wish you were a little more aware.'"

DIFFERENT PEOPLE,
DIFFERENT DREAMS

Tim: I grew up in a time not that long ago but in a world that no longer exists. I remember a white split-level home in suburban St. Louis on an acre and a half of zoysia as soft as a down comforter. I remember a mother who lived to serve her family and a father who was strict and severe and emotionally absent. I remember walking to school, coming home without homework, and simply telling my mother, "I'm going out." "Out where?" "To play." I rode my bike on busy streets without a helmet and carried a pocketknife wherever I went—even to school. What I loved most about my childhood is that I was free.

Joy: I grew up in Columbus, Ohio, in a neighborhood where every child belonged to every family. We spent every summer day together at the neighborhood pool, and through the year we all walked together to school and back. We walked home for lunch as well—we walked through the woods, through places I would never allow my children to walk today. But my parents never had to worry if I would make it home each day, because, above all, my neighborhood was safe.

Tim: There are things about my childhood I loved, and things I despised. There are parts of my early days that I long to reproduce in my own family, and things I'll do most anything to avoid. The irony is, I'm not always sure what those things are; they live invisibly inside me, lurking in the background, operating not as specific goals but as indefinable longings—as dreams. Like post-hypnotic suggestions, they inform all my conscious actions, though I'm seldom aware they even exist. As I grew up, I collected a series of fuzzy mental images of how my life would look one day. How it should look. I had a dream.

Joy: When we got married, Tim naturally expected that his wife would share not only his tastes and opinions but his dreams as well. What he never counted on is that I would have dreams of my own—very different dreams. This difference in our mental images, this disparity in our "shoulds" and "oughts," was what originally attracted us to each other. But in marriage, the same differences became the source of many of our disagreements. He had his dreams, and I had mine.

It took us quite awhile to understand that our biggest conflicts would come when we were both right.

The Battle of Dreams

We all have dreams—fuzzy mental images of how our lives are supposed to look and feel. Marital researcher Scott Stanley calls these unconscious longings *hidden issues*. "Hidden issues," he writes, "are the deeper, fundamental issues that usually lie underneath the arguments about issues and events. . . . For all too many couples, the hidden issues never come out. They fester and produce fear, sadness, and resentment that can erode and eventually destroy the marriage."

The author's solution? "The most important thing you can do is simply to talk about these hidden issues constructively, perhaps at a time set aside just for this purpose."[1]

> **INSIGHT**
> You don't get harmony when everybody sings the same note.
> —*Doug Floyd*

Good advice, but easier said than done. The problem with hidden issues is precisely that—they're *hidden.* How do you locate the Invisible Man? You can blow smoke at him and look for the hole he leaves, or you can shine a light on him and search for his shadow. But you don't discover his presence directly; you only become aware of him through something he *affects.* A hidden issue is almost impossible to spot until something comes along to reveal its contours.

That "something" is usually conflict.

Christians are inadvertently taught to avoid conflict. The apostle Peter tells us, "All of you be harmonious, sympathetic, brotherly, kind-hearted, and humble in spirit" (1 Peter 3:8). Paul admonished Christians to be "like-minded, having the same love, being one in spirit and purpose" (Philippians 2:2 NIV). Doesn't it follow, then, that the ideal marriage is one that lacks conflict of any kind?

The simplest conflicts are the disagreements where one of you is just plain *wrong*. You got the facts wrong, or you forgot, or—to be honest—you just didn't care. Though we sometimes fight even when we know we're wrong, our better side usually gets the best of us and sooner or later we own up to it. *Sorry about that. I was wrong, you were right.*

The more difficult conflicts—the ones that we'll describe in this book—are the ones in which you're *both* right. These disagreements are harder to resolve because neither one of you wants to let go—but then, neither one of you needs to. At its worst, conflict is when you demonstrate your selfishness, arrogance, and sheer mule-headedness. But at its best, *conflict is when you both express what you really believe in—and, in the process, come to a better understanding of one another.*

INSIGHT

The value of marriage is not that adults produce children, but that children produce adults.

—*Peter de Vries*

Throughout our married life, we have often disagreed in our approach to raising our kids. Joy thought our son should wear his bicycle helmet to simply ride around the block; Tim thought it was an unnecessary nuisance for such a short distance. Joy thought we should remind the kids to take a jacket when they went out; Tim thought they should learn to remember for themselves, and a little frostbite just might do the trick. Joy thought we should install Internet filtering software on our home computer to protect the kids from accidentally going to inappropriate sites; Tim thought the kids should know that the sites were there, but develop the self-control to not visit them. At times, we seemed to disagree about *everything*.

Over time, we began to recognize the outline of the Invisible Man. We began to realize that our individual disagreements were like the leaves on a tree, obscuring the trunk behind it. Our disagreements about helmets and jackets and software were all the result of a *single fundamental difference between us.* When it came to the children, Joy instinctively placed their security above all else, and Tim instinctively valued their *autonomy*—their need to take risks in order to grow in confidence and capability.

What could possibly be wrong with valuing a child's security? What could be wrong with wanting to raise a child in such a way that she actually *survives* childhood?

And what could be wrong with valuing a child's autonomy? What could be wrong with teaching a child to take reasonable risks, to begin to prepare him for the time when he'll be making decisions on his own?

There's nothing wrong with either perspective. The problem was that each of us instinctively approached all child-rearing decisions from our own perspective—the "right" perspective. Neither of us could explain exactly *why* our perspective was right—but then, why should we have to? Isn't it obvious?

Joy's perspective is much more than her opinion; it's her *dream.* Joy's mental image is a photograph of children who are first and foremost safe and warm, sheltered from the elements, protected from all the very real dangers that threaten children today.

That's an excellent dream.

But Tim's dream is of children who are first of all *free,* risk takers who think for themselves, take responsibility for their own lives, and bounce back quickly from adversity.

That's a good dream too.

They're both good dreams, but how in the world do you combine them? When one partner wants to push the birds out of the nest and the other wants to protect them from hitting the ground, what do you do?

There's an easy solution to our conflict—one of us could just give in. But what would be the implications for the kids if we completely neglected the value of security? Would we still *have* any children? And what would be the long-term impact on the kids if we ignored the value of autonomy, the goal of teaching them to stand on their own two feet?

The problem is that we're *both* right.

It took years of lengthy "discussions" before we finally realized two critical things: that we were not really battling about bicycle helmets and jackets and computers at all, and that *we were really on the same side.* We just chose different paths to a common goal: a mature and thriving child.

Once we understood that the issue of Security was the underlying cause of many of our disagreements, we began to search for other hidden causes. Was it possible that there were more fundamental issues like this, more instinctive blind spots that were the root of our other disagreements?

INSIGHT
The home is not the one tame place in the world of adventure. It is the one wild place in the world of rules and set tasks.
—*G. K. Chesterton*

13

Sure enough, others began to emerge, and after many more discussions we were finally able to identify seven fundamental differences between us.

Then we began to discuss our conclusions with other couples and ask if they had observed a similar phenomenon in their own marriages. We asked each couple, "Are there recurring areas of conflict in your marriage—areas that you seem to come back to over and over again? Are there topics you *can almost predict* you'll disagree on?" In each case, we encouraged them to try to identify what they were *really* fighting about.

To our surprise, we found that other couples had recurring disagreements over the very same seven issues we did.

Our next step was to test our theory with a larger audience. Over the next two years, as we traveled and spoke at marriage conferences across the country, we began to take a survey with our audiences. We asked more than a thousand couples a series of questions about their own experience with conflict, and wherever we went our findings were consistent. We discovered that there seem to be seven common underlying issues that are the root cause of most of the conflict in married life.

We call them *Security, Loyalty, Responsibility, Caring, Order, Openness*, and *Connection*.

One of Us Must Be Crazy

By this time in your marriage, the two of you have probably negotiated and compromised on an exhausting number of minor preferences and desires. But have you noticed that a handful of stubborn disagreements still remain, and that those issues seem to crop up again and again with discouraging regularity? Like ancient Rome, all roads lead to them. No matter what topic begins the disagreement, sooner or later you find yourselves on familiar ground. "Oh no, not *this* again!"

Recurring conflicts are a reality for all married couples, and they are a source of ongoing frustration and discouragement. Their very existence is annoying. Couples feel they should have resolved their differences by this time, and their failure to do so must mean something is wrong between them.

Not at all.

INSIGHT

A happy home is one in which each spouse grants the possibility that the other may be right, though neither believes it.

—*Don Fraser*

INSIGHT

Everything that irritates us about others can lead us to an understanding of ourselves.

—*Carl Jung*

Psychologist John Gottman is a relationship expert who has studied the conflict styles of married couples for many years. He believes that all marital conflicts fall into one of two categories. "Either they can be resolved," he writes, "or they are perpetual, which means they will be a part of your lives forever, in some form or another."[2]

Gottman estimates that almost 70 percent of marital conflicts are *perpetual*. "The majority of marital problems fall into this category—69 percent, to be exact. Time and again when we do four-year follow-ups of couples, we find that they are still arguing about precisely the same issue. It's as if four minutes have passed rather than four years."[3]

If Gottman is correct, only three out of ten marital disagreements will have a neat and tidy solution. The rest, like some alien shape-shifter, will return to visit us again and again in some unexpected form.

Couples often wonder if these unresolved issues reveal some secret weakness in their partner or their marriage. Each begins to suspect the other of immaturity, pride, or sheer pigheadedness. They know that whenever the subject shifts to one of *those* topics, there will be no resolution. They will end up, as always, in an angry stalemate, burying the disagreement like toxic waste until it surfaces again another day.

Our first disagreements in marriage are over a wide variety of issues as we adjust to each other and to married life. We gradually resolve these issues until only the more confusing and difficult ones remain. Finally, after several years we whittle down our areas of disagreement to a handful that just won't seem to go away—the ones that really matter to us. These issues are far more than opinions or even values—they are a part of the way we see the world itself. Over the years, as we express our differences and resolve them, we engage in a kind of pruning process: First we cut away twigs, then branches, then limbs, until we finally come to the trunk of the tree itself.

All of us have dreams—fundamental convictions about how life and love and marriage *ought* to work. Our convictions tell us what's good and bad, right and wrong, fair and unjust. They are the operating system of our computer; they work behind the scenes, invisible, but always running in the background. They are the result of gender differences, environmental influences, and individual temperament—but

SIX approaches to reconciling our dreams that never work

1.
Trying to talk her out of her dreams, or into yours

2.
Accusing him of being irrational because his dream doesn't make sense to you

3.
Arguing the greater virtue, logic, or practical benefit of your dream

4.
Accusing her of overreacting because her dream means too much to her

5.
Identifying five friends who do things your way

6.
Accusing him of just being stubborn

INSIGHT

No one has completed his education who has not learned to live with an insoluble problem.

—*Edmund J. Keifer*

regardless of the source, by the time we are adults, they are so intimate a part of us that we are no more aware of them than we are the blinking of our eyes.

And that's the problem. We all assume that we are marrying someone just like us, with similar opinions and values and tastes, unaware that far below the surface there may reside a worldview that differs from our own at significant points—and these differences tend to surface in conflict. Sometimes a conflict is more than a simple disagreement—it's a virtual clash of worldviews, and the disagreement appears impossible to resolve because it seems inconceivable to consider the issue from any other perspective than the one you *know* to be correct. Thus the title of our book: *One of us must be crazy . . . and I'm pretty sure it's you*.

When we lose hope of ever really *resolving* our deepest differences, they become the "no-man's-land" of marriage. We constantly check ourselves: *Careful—don't go there*. We begin to fence off those areas of the relationship where no one dares to tread—but we do this at a great price. The benefit of this approach is peace, or at least the absence of conflict, but the price of this evasion is the very thing we want most from marriage—true intimacy.

Understanding the Differences That Divide

But what's the point in discussing all this? Aren't these hidden issues what John Gottman described as "perpetual"? Because of our fundamental differences, aren't we doomed to repeat these disagreements over and over again in different forms? And if they won't go away, why bother to talk about them at all?

The reason we need to talk about the issues of *Security, Loyalty, Responsibility, Caring, Order, Openness, and Connection* is precisely *because* they won't go away. They're always there, and they always *matter*. Your different approaches to these issues represent much more than differences of opinion; it's a battle of dreams, and dreams die hard.

If you feel like having Italian food for dinner but your mate prefers Chinese, you might be merely disappointed; but if you have a deep, pervasive longing to build a safe, secure home, and your mate is not cooperating, you'll be much more than disappointed. "Hope deferred makes the heart sick," Proverbs 13:12 tells us, and these hidden issues are exactly that—deeply held hopes that are deferred or sometimes denied altogether by our partner, the very person we feel should most share our dreams. When these seven underlying issues are simply avoided and left to fester, they can produce an underlying atmosphere of anger, bitterness, and resentment. No wonder Scott Stanley says, "Hidden issues often drive our most frustrating and destructive arguments."[4]

But if we do talk about them, since they're not going to just disappear, what can we really hope to accomplish? Perhaps the best way to answer this question is by telling you what understanding these differences did for *us*.

First, it helped us to *identify our dreams*. Remember, dreams are often hidden issues. It would be very helpful in a marriage if a husband would simply say to his wife, "I should warn you that I'm extremely sensitive about issues of Loyalty. It's a dream of mine to have an unwaveringly loyal wife."

Unfortunately, he may be consciously unaware of his sensitivity altogether; he might not even be aware of what Loyalty really entails, as we'll discuss later. But just wait until the first argument about the in-laws—then the dream will go to work, lurking in the background, fueling the anger and confusion and frustration. The problem is that this husband and wife may go on forever believing that they're fighting about the in-laws, never recognizing that the underlying concern is really all about *Loyalty*. Identifying our underlying differences allows us to ignore the diversion created by a hundred minor disagreements and talk about the real issue. "What do you long for? What is your mental image of how marriage ought to be? What does a husband look like to you? How do you think kids should be raised? Tell me about your dreams."

Second, understanding our hidden issues helped us to *put our differences in perspective*. When it came to rearing the kids, one moment we thought that we disagreed about *everything*, from allowances to curfews to appropriate forms of discipline. Suddenly we understood that we only disagreed about *one* thing, but that one issue influenced our approach to dozens of others. That understanding alone changed

> ## The Word
> There are three things that amaze me—no, four things that I don't understand: How an eagle glides through the sky, How a snake slithers on a rock, How a ship navigates the ocean, How a man loves a woman.
>
> PROVERBS 30:18–19 NLT

our self-perception, from a couple who could never seem to agree, to a couple with only a handful of fundamental differences. That change in perspective allowed us to shift our focus from the superficial symptoms to the underlying disease.

Third, understanding our hidden issues helped us to *understand each other's true motives*. Joy was concerned about the children's safety, but Tim didn't seem to care if they got hurt. Tim wanted the kids to grow to independence, but Joy seemed to want to keep them tied to her apron strings. The other's perspective seemed so selfish and short-sighted that it naturally produced anger in each of us. *Why don't you care what happens to the kids?* We both cared, of course; we both wanted the best for the kids, but that was hard to believe.

Psychologists Clifford Notarius and Howard Markman call this problem *hot thoughts*. "All too often we tend to think the worst about our partner rather than the best," they write. "When you latch on to the worst possible explanations for your partner's behavior, you're going to make your partner *and* yourself feel miserable."[5] Understanding the underlying conflict allowed us to eliminate our "hot thoughts" by seeing the other's motives in a completely different light.

Fourth, understanding our hidden issues helped us to *anticipate conflicts before they occurred*. As we said earlier, couples learn which topics are most likely to generate a conflict and "rope off" those areas as if they were minefields. But the problem with a minefield is that the dangers lie buried, so the explosions are often unexpected. We begin by discussing bicycle helmets, and before we know it, it's a full-fledged argument. How did *that* happen? Once we understood each other's underlying dreams, we could look for other issues that might be influenced by those same dreams. That allowed us to take a *proactive* approach to our differences rather than always having to clean up messes and bandage wounds later on. We knew where we were likely to disagree, and we could be ready for it.

Finally, understanding our hidden issues helped us to *work together as partners* instead of battling as foes. Once we understood each other's dreams, once we each realized what the other person was valuing, our attitudes changed. We wanted to help fulfill the other's dreams rather than stubbornly defend our own turf. That change in attitude has allowed us to work together as partners instead of constantly shouting at each other from opposite sides of the fence.

Dreaming Together

In the chapters that follow, we'll describe in detail the seven fundamental differences that divide us in marriage. We'll illustrate each issue from our own marriage, and we'll offer some of the insights and ideas from the hundreds of couples who responded to our survey. We'll help you identify where you and your mate stand in relation to each issue—and, more important, where you stand in relation to each other.

We'll encourage you to consider both the assets and the potential liabilities of the dreams of Security, Loyalty, Responsibility, Caring, Order, Openness, and Connection. Each of these dreams can be an excellent ambition, but each can have a dark side too—a dark side that can be avoided when we seek to achieve balance and avoid extremes.

> **INSIGHT**
> The art of living lies less in eliminating our troubles than in growing with them.
> —*Bernard M. Baruch*

For each issue, we'll give you two practical principles to help you begin to dream together—one tip for the spouse who holds the dream and one for the spouse who doesn't. We'll recommend fresh approaches in substance *and* style to maximize your chances for making new headway in each area.

Dreams die hard, but your dreams don't have to die at all. The presence of conflict in your marriage is not a condemnation. It simply means that you have *dreams*—that you are human beings and that there are things you long for, things you truly believe in. The question is, how will you believe in them *together*? How will you honor each other's dreams, even when they sometimes conflict? You know what to do when one of you is wrong; what will you do when both of you are right?

SECURITY

Loyalty

Responsibility

Caring

Order

Openness

Connection

THE DIFFERENCES THAT DIVIDE

"Nonsense! I never wore a bicycle helmet when I was a boy."

1 SECURITY:

PROTECTION and PROVISION

Tim: Our son Tommy learned to ride a bicycle without training wheels at the glorious age of three. I couldn't have been prouder.

Joy: I was proud of him, too, but three was a little early. I wanted him to be safe.

Tim: To see my son racing off down the sidewalk at only three was a real thrill for me. It was a part of my dream—kids who were free to go where they want, when they want. As I said in the last chapter, I grew up with a lot of freedom myself.

Joy: Sure, Tim had a lot of freedom, but what he's not telling you is that he's only alive today because of the sheer grace of God. Did he mention that he once set his pants on fire by mounting model rockets to his handlebars?

Tim: Batman's bike had those. It was very cool.

Joy: I imagine all the moms grabbing their children when Tim went riding by, scrambling into the house, and bolting all the doors. He had more visits to the emergency room in his first six years of life than Jackie Chan.

Tim: It was mostly for head injuries. Believe me, Joy's gotten a lot of mileage out of that.

Joy: Tim once burned down two of his father's prize evergreens in their front yard. He once shot a hole in his father's shoulder with a bottle rocket gone astray.

Tim: Now that you mention it, Dad did seem to be angry a lot.

Joy: I could write pages. When I grew up, I had a mother who always knew where I was going and who I'd be playing with. Is it any wonder that with Tim's history of freedom and independence, I would value security more than he does? I didn't go through twenty-one hours of labor with Tommy just to have him perish in his first adventure with his dad.

The Two Sides of Security

In your own marriage, one of you will instinctively place a higher value on *Security*. Security is the need to be safe, the desire to know that you and yours are first of all protected from harm. Several responses from our survey revealed a desire for Security . . .

- *I like to spend, and she likes to save.*

- *When we have a major purchase, he wants to buy new and the most expensive quality. I would prefer to spend less but still get the job done.*

- *I want to feel secure—in his love, in my home, in our marriage, with him versus his family, financially—and I would like him to lead us spiritually (I long for this).*

- *Why does he feel the need to spend the extra money we have instead of saving it?*

- *I always wait until he's in bed and then I double-check the door, because sometimes he forgets to lock it.*

- *Why am I always the one who tucks the kids in at night?*

- *Why does he have to save everything? Why can't he throw anything away?*

Dangers come in many forms—physical and emotional, real and imagined—and so the dream of Security is a tree that puts out many branches. There are two chief offshoots from this tree: the desire for *Protection* and the desire for *Provision*.

Protection: Safety First

Protection in its most basic form is the instinct for survival, but it covers a lot more. Protection also includes the longing for safety, stability, and even comfort. Commercials that air at Christmastime show families snuggled together around the fireplace, images of warmth and love and Security. A protected family is one that has everything it needs to be safe, warm, dry, and happy.

Provision: Preparing for Future Needs

Provision is the desire to make sure everyone has enough, a desire that makes it necessary to both collect and save. Provision is concerned not only about the present but the future. Sure, we have enough *now*—but what about tomorrow? "Look at an ant," Proverbs advises us. "Watch it closely; let it teach you a thing or two. Nobody has to tell it what to do. All summer it stores up food; at harvest it stockpiles provisions" (6:6–8 THE MESSAGE). If you value Security, this may be your life verse.

Because Security looks to the future, it would rather save than spend. "Do we have to spend that much? It would be nice—but if we spend it today, we won't have it tomorrow."

Because Security wants to provide, it would rather collect than throw away. "I know we no longer need this, but what if we get rid of it and then we need it again? If we save it, we *have* it, and it'll be there just in case."

Because Security wants to protect, it has an aversion to risk. "Why do you want to try that? There are a lot safer things we can do that are just as fun." It isn't that the one who dreams of Security doesn't want to have fun—it's just that she's valuing something more. A dream isn't simply a matter of preference; a dream is a nonnegotiable, an essential priority. She's willing to take risks, to seek adventure, and to seize the day—as long as everyone is safe. Security comes *first*.

By the way, in case you're getting the wrong idea here, the dream of Security isn't gender specific. We don't mean to suggest that men are always the risk takers while women are always seeking to Protect and Provide. Our dreams are influenced by our family of origin, our built-in temperament, and the culture around us. Men who were born in the Great Depression era are often far more security oriented than men *and* women of later generations—and today's difficult economy can produce the same effect. If your childhood home was unstable, you may have an increased desire for Security as an adult. If your childhood home was especially warm and secure, you may long to reproduce that environment in your own home. It's difficult, if not impossible, to ascribe our deepest longings to a single cause. The point here is

> **INSIGHT**
>
> Take calculated risks. That's not the same as being in a rush.
>
> —*General George Patton*

that either one of you may have the dream of Security.

But there is one variable that tends to tip the scale of Security toward women—the arrival of children. As Joy said earlier, "I didn't go through twenty-one hours of labor with Tommy just to have him perish in his first adventure with his dad." Women have a greater original investment in children, and they often sense that the greater burden of the children's Security continues to be theirs. Marriage is where life gets serious—but parenting is where life gets critical. Children are like a lens that focuses and magnifies the fears and longings of parents. We value our own Security, but we can get frantic about our children's safety. We may have only a minor desire for Security as a single person or as a young married, but when children come along, we sometimes find that our minor desire has blossomed into a full-blown passion.

INSIGHT

S-A-F-E is spelled D-U-L-L.

—*Alan Clark*

Differing Priorities

Security comes at a price. It often requires you to limit your freedom in some way—and that's how the argument begins. If Protection and Provision are not your natural priorities, then your Security-minded partner can seem like a killjoy. Why can't he lighten up? Why can't he stop worrying about everything? You have to take *some* risks, or what's the point of being alive?

But if Security is your priority, then your risk-taking partner seems just plain irresponsible. After all, it's *safety* we're talking about here, and surely that comes before everything else. Fun is good, risk is good, but let's not get carried away. We are *responsible* here. Let's not enjoy today at tomorrow's expense.

When you discuss these issues in your own marriage—and you undoubtedly do—you may have never realized that it's Security you've been discussing all along. That's because Security is a *hidden* issue, remember? We fail to recognize the Security issue as such because it comes to us in the form of a dozen smaller, seemingly unrelated arguments. They don't look like conflicts about Security—they look like arguments about money and irresponsibility and overprotecting the kids. The goal is to look behind the *apparent* disagreement and ask, "What are we *really* fighting about here?"

Let's observe a few disagreements from the marriages of couples we've interviewed and see if you can spot the root of *Security* underneath.

> *He:*   *Isn't this a great vacation?*
>
> *She:* *Yeah. Great.*
>
> *He:*   *How did you like the parasailing? Wasn't that incredible?*
>
> *She:* *Uh-huh. How much did that cost, anyway?*
>
> *He:*   *Only forty bucks.*
>
> *She:* *Each?*
>
> *He:*   *It was worth it. Where do you want to go for dinner tonight?*
>
> *She:* *I was thinking maybe I could cook tonight. There's a little kitchenette in the room . . .*
>
> *He:*   *What's your problem, anyway?*
>
> *She:* *What problem?*
>
> *He:*   *I went all out to plan this vacation—first-class airfare, beachfront hotel room, four-star restaurants—and all you do is drag your feet.*
>
> *She:* *Does everything have to be so . . . expensive?*
>
> *He:*   *There you go again! You never want to have fun anymore.*

The husband in the scenario above thinks they're disagreeing about their approaches to fun. He fears that his wife no longer wants to be his recreational partner, something that's very important to him. *She's no fun anymore. . . . Maybe she's getting older. Maybe she's just getting dull! Before long all she'll want to do is lie around the house and watch TV.*

He might also conclude that they're fighting about money. *All she wants to do is hoard money! What's the point in saving money if you never get a chance to **spend** any of it? We're not going to be young forever. By the time she's ready to spend some money, we'll be too old to enjoy it.*

But they aren't disagreeing about having fun, and they're not disagreeing about money. Those are just the *apparent* conflicts. Underneath it all, they're arguing about Security. She needs to know that this no-limits vacation won't put them in debt for the rest of their lives. She wants to enjoy the present, too, but not at the expense of the future—not at the expense of *Security*.

He: *Look what I found in the trash can. Our toaster!*

She: *It's our **old** toaster.*

He: *You weren't going to throw it away, were you?*

She: *Of course. We just bought a brand-new one.*

He: *But it still works. Look, I'll plug it in . . . See?*

She: *Why would we save the old toaster when we have a brand-new one? We don't need two toasters.*

He: *What if the new one breaks? It's good to have a backup.*

She: *Greg, our attic is **filled** with "backups."*

He: *Why would you throw away a perfectly good toaster?*

She: *If it was "perfectly good," why in the world did we buy a **new** one?*

He: *I just don't like to waste things. I guess **my** family didn't have money to burn like **yours** did.*

The husband's desire to save a worn-out toaster even after they've bought a new one seems downright irrational to his wife—and he has a hard time explaining it himself. He tries to offer a logical rationale—the need for a backup, the moral responsibility not to be wasteful—but deep inside, all he knows for sure is that it *feels* wrong. He doesn't want a toaster; he wants Security. If one toaster breaks, now they have another. They're *Protected*. Now they can *Provide*, even if it's only half-browned toast.

But the argument is about to get ugly. In his desperation to provide a rational explanation for his desire, he suggests that it's really all his *wife's* problem. His wife is *wasteful*, and, worse than that, she picked up the bad habit from her family. "The best defense is a good offense," the old saying goes, and this man has put it into practice. But he has forgotten another ancient piece of wisdom: "A gentle answer turns away wrath, but a harsh word stirs up anger" (Proverbs 15:1).

This couple couldn't see the forest for the trees, and now they may spend the rest of the evening arguing about anything *but* Security.

She: *Alex forgot his umbrella again.*

He: *You're kidding. Again?*

She: *Now I'm going to have to drop it off at his school.*

He: *Why?*

She: Because it's supposed to rain this afternoon, that's why. I don't want him to get soaked to the bone on the way home.

He: Anne, we live a hundred yards from the bus stop.

She: It's far enough to get drenched. I don't want him to catch a cold.

He: Stop coddling him. Let him catch a cold; it's the only way he's going to learn to take his umbrella.

She: And when he catches a cold, who's going to take care of him all day? Not you, that's for sure. I swear, I don't think you'd put him out if he was on fire.

Conflicts over Security can be difficult because, to both partners, the issue seems so *obvious.* To her, the argument boils down to: *I care about the kids' welfare and you don't.* For him, the bottom line is: *If you don't stop babying the kids, they'll never grow up.* Both have good goals in mind— good *dreams*—but they're approaching the situation from opposite sides. They see the flaws in their partner's position, but they're completely unaware of their own blind spots. *Why doesn't he care about Alex? Why won't she stop smothering him?*

To make matters worse, the husband just used a loaded word. "Stop *coddling* him," he said. The word means "to treat indulgently; to baby." His wife doesn't need a dictionary to know what it means—and she knows exactly what he's intending by it. In response, she suggests that his attitude is not only callous but selfish, since she is the one who will have to take care of the sick child. It's easy to be the risk taker when you're not the one who has to pay the price for it.

This couple began by talking about a forgotten umbrella, but in less than one minute they arrived at the root of the conflict, the issue of Security. The argument is a familiar one, but they've never been able to give it a name. They disagree, but they're not really sure what they're disagreeing *about.*

> **INSIGHT**
> You can't put a price tag on love, but you can on all its accessories.

She: Here's one more bag. We need to put this in too.

He: Jane, we're only going away for three days. You've packed enough stuff to last us a month!

She: We've still got some room. You can squeeze it in over there.

He: That's not the point. (Pokes at the bag) What is all this stuff?

She: (Crossly) Things we need.

He: We can't possibly need all this. Just once I wish we would set a one-bag limit. One bag for each of us, and that's it.

She: And what would you do when you got there and you forgot something?

He: I'd just do without it. Or I'd go to the store and buy it.

She: You'd go to the store and buy things we already own. Now **that** makes sense. Stop making such a fuss over a few suitcases.

He: That's easy for you to say; you don't have to fit it all in the trunk.

Every time they prepare for a trip, they end up in an argument. She overpacks—at least *he* thinks so. Each time a vacation approaches, he tells himself that *this* time he's just going to bite his lip and hold his tongue—but there always seems to be "one more bag" that sends him over the edge and sets the argument in motion.

He wants his wife to explain the need for "all this stuff." She is not about to have to justify every item she's packed. She wants to make sure that wherever they go and whatever circumstances arise, they will have everything they need. At this point, he would just as soon go naked and hungry—at least until he needs something she brought, and then he's glad she packed it.

He would have a hard time explaining why this situation bothers him so much. He dreams of a vacation where he doesn't have to bother with all this. His wife reminds him that if he doesn't bother with it, he won't *have* it. "That's okay with me," her husband would say. "Maybe it's okay *now*," she would respond, "but wait until you don't have it."

When it comes time for vacation, he just wants to *go*. She wants to go too—she just wants Security to go with them.

Do you recognize yourself or your mate in any of the scenarios above? They typify four areas where the dream of Security commonly surfaces. We could discuss many more, but now it's time to see how *you* relate to the issue of Security. Consider the following questions, and decide whether each one is truer of you or your mate . . .

"Folks, this is an electronics store. Male-to-female adapters don't work on people."

SECURITY INVENTORY—Protection	YOU	MATE
Who always thinks to make sure the kids are warm enough?		
Who is more likely to stay awake during a severe storm?		
Who is more willing to go parasailing or rappelling and take the kids along too?		
Who would rather block the bad channels on the cable TV or not get cable at all?		
Who would rather install Internet monitoring or blocking software?		
Who asks more often where the child is going and with whom?		
Who calls a child's teacher about a mistreatment or confusion in the child's classroom?		
Who always has his or her eye on the younger child?		

SECURITY INVENTORY—Provision	YOU	MATE
Who is more eager to save for the future?		
Who is more concerned about a financial plan for retirement or college?		
Who wants to make sure that the details of a trip are taken care of?		
Who makes sure that the family always has what it needs before going somewhere?		
Who saves things for some future use?		
Who is more concerned with providing a way for the child to make friends or get involved?		
Who thinks most about the family's material, social, or spiritual needs?		

Finding the Root

On a scale from one to ten, how important is Security to you? Place an X where you think you belong. Now put an O where you think your mate belongs.

1   10

Are there recurring arguments in your marriage that you think might be driven by the desire for Security? What are they about?

Do you think there is something from your past that makes your desire for Security especially important to you? Have you ever discussed this with your mate?

Do you think there is something happening in your life right now that could be heightening your desire for Security?

Dreaming Together: Security

The desire for Protection and Provision is an excellent dream—but when it goes too far, the dream has a dark side too.

THE **GOOD** SIDE OF SECURITY	THE **DARK** SIDE OF SECURITY
Safety	A fear of all risk-taking
Being well-equipped	Being overloaded
Minimizing risk	Minimizing options
Forethought and planning	Failing to trust in God's provision
Thinking of the future	Failing to enjoy today
Secure children	Overprotected children
Anticipating problems	Fear, worry, and anxiety
Spouse who feels protected	Spouse who feels limited

A Tip for Spouses of the Security-Minded

If Security is not your natural concern, what can you do to help satisfy your mate's greater desire for Protection and Provision? You can *address Security before mentioning risk*.

We have a friend who once raced home to bring his wife some exciting news. All the way home he imagined her response—first her disbelief, then her gradual, astonished realization, and finally her overwhelming joy. He barely made it in the door before he blurted out the news.

"Guess what!" he said. "We're going to *China*!"

His wife just stood there, staring at him.

"Did you hear what I said? We're going to China for *two weeks*!"

There was a long pause, and then his wife slowly said, "What about the kids? Can they come too? We can't just leave them—who could take care of them for two weeks? What about the dog? And who would take care of our house? It's the middle of the summer—someone would have to water the grass."

This time it was his turn to stare. "I can't believe you," he said. "I tell you that we have a chance to visit China, and all you can think about is watering the grass."

But she wasn't thinking about the grass—she was thinking about Security. She could be excited about the news, too, just as soon as she was sure that Protection and Provision were taken care of. China is great, but Security comes first.

Our friend realized later that he could have made things much easier for his wife if he had addressed her desires for Security *before* he brought up a potential risk. He might have said something more like this:

"I have some great news for you! I want you to know that this will affect the kids, and the dog, and the house—but I also want you to know that I've thought about all these things and we can take care of them. I know someone who can watch the kids, and I've taken care of the dog, and I've got the house covered. Are you ready? We're going to China!"

She may still have had *some* hesitation, and she still might have needed time to process all her concerns—but her husband would have gotten a lot better response if he had used this approach. The next time you want to suggest an activity that involves some risk—however slight the risk might appear to *you*—ask yourself, "Before I bring this up, how can I address my mate's desire for Security *first*?"

Let's revisit one of the scenarios from this chapter to see how this principle might have made a difference. Remember the husband and wife who were trying to enjoy a vacation together? *He* was enjoying himself, but *she* was not.

> He: *Isn't this a great vacation?*
> She: *Yeah. Great.*
> He: *How did you like the parasailing? Wasn't that incredible?*
> She: *Uh-huh. How much did that cost, anyway?*

Suppose instead that this husband applied the principle of *addressing Security before mentioning risk.* The conversation might have gone more like this:

INSIGHT

A family vacation is one where you arrive with five bags, four kids, and seven I-thought-you-packed-its.

—*Ivern Ball*

> He: *Isn't this a great vacation?*
>
> She: *Yeah. Great.*
>
> He: *Look, I know that you're concerned about the finances. I want you to know that I've already thought it all through.*
>
> She: *You have?*
>
> He: *Yes, and I even made up a budget for us. I'd like us to do some things that are really different, even a little pricey—but I want you to know that we can afford it, and we're not going to have to go into debt. We can afford this.*

The wife would have been able to enjoy herself much more if her husband had first addressed the financial plan for the vacation. By addressing Security first, he could make it possible for her to be more comfortable with risk.

A Tip for the Security-Minded

If Protection and Provision are your instinctive dream, how can you maintain balance and avoid the dark side of Security? One good way for the Security-minded to accommodate the dream of her risk-taking partner is by *creating pockets of acceptable risk.*

The desire for complete Security can lead to a fear of *all* risk-taking. Without *some* openness to uncertainty, no one would ever have children, change jobs, make an investment, or travel more than a few miles from home. It all involves risk. We want our risk-taking partners to feel the freedom to dream dreams and shoot for the stars, but we want our families to be safe too. We want them to feel protected, but not chained to the bed.

INSIGHT

The best security blanket a child can have is parents who respect each other.

— *Jan Blaustone*

Those who value Security can't be expected to simply "lighten up," but they *can* look for areas in which they can feel free to resist the natural impulse toward Protection and Provision. These areas must be *within an overall safe environment*—that's why we call them *pockets of acceptable risk.*

Suppose that the Security-minded wife in our scenario had approached the vacation with our principle of *creating pockets of acceptable risk*. Their conversation might have sounded more like this:

He: *Isn't this a great vacation?*

She: *Yeah. Can I make a suggestion, though? There's one way you could help me enjoy this vacation a lot more.*

He: *Really? How?*

She: *You know that I worry about our finances sometimes. Could we take a few minutes to decide how much we're going to spend on this vacation?*

He: *(Groan) You want to know what everything costs?*

She: *Not everything—just a bottom-line number, whatever we agree we can afford. After that, as long as we stay under that number, anything goes.*

He may still resist the idea of having to make a budget—but he would change his mind if he could see what a difference this simple step would make in his wife's attitude. Of course, it's better for both of them if they do this step *before* they go on vacation, but at this point the wife has realized the vacation is costing more than she thought it would, and she's finding it hard to relax and enjoy it. She can't ignore her desire for Security, but if she knows that they at least have a bottom line, then she's created a *pocket of acceptable risk*. Within that pocket, she could feel free to take a few chances—much to her husband's delight.

Security

LOYALTY

Responsibility

Caring

Order

Openness

Connection

"You might as well stop pretending, John. I know when your eyes are wandering."

2 LOYALTY:

FAITHFULNESS and PRIORITY

Tim: Not long ago I got together with some old buddies of mine. We went to a friend's beach house for the weekend, just the four of us. Just the guys.

Joy: Which I think is great.

Tim: We started talking about how we all met each other for the first time. My friend Kent remembered the first time we ever met, and I could remember the first time I ever saw him. We went around the table, sharing our memories, until we came to my friend Mike. He recounted our first meeting, and then everyone turned to me and waited—but I just sat there. Finally Mike said, "You mean to tell me you can't remember anything about the first time we met?" I said, "Oh, please—I get enough of that from my wife."

Joy: This is why women worry about men in groups.

Tim: It was a funny line. Everybody howled! Mike thought it was such a great joke that when he got back with me, he shared it with Joy. Guess what? Joy didn't think it was funny.

Joy: Can you imagine that?

Tim: Joy thought that my little joke was at her expense. I told her, "I wasn't laughing at you, honey; I was laughing with you."

Joy: And I explained to him that to be laughing with someone, two people have to be laughing.

Tim: I told Joy that it was no big deal—that sometimes when men get together, they make little jokes about their wives.

Joy: I said I know. Sometimes wives do the same thing—and whenever their husbands hear about it later, it bothers them—and it should.

Tim: I finally began to understand why it mattered to her. It was more than a joke at Joy's expense; it was an act of disloyalty. I had said something in private that I would never have said in her presence. I had painted a picture of her that was less than flattering—a stereotype of a nagging, demanding wife that wasn't true of her at all. Instead of defending Joy, I was demeaning her—and I was doing it behind her back.

Joy: Every wife wants to know that she can trust her husband, not just in the big things but in the little things as well. She wants to know that her husband is loyal—not only in what he says to her but in what he says about her.

Tim: So I learned a good lesson. And I told Mike that I still couldn't remember the first time we met, but I sure would remember the last.

Dreaming of Loyalty

Loyalty is the value that asks, "Whose side are you on, anyway?" It's the dream of a partner who is a true *soul mate*—someone who is unreservedly committed to you and to the relationship. Consider some comments from our survey that indicate that the dream of Loyalty is at work . . .

- *We repeatedly disagree over outside obligations coming before me.*

- *He takes a piece of my heart with every lie.*

- *Why can't he stand up to his father on his family's behalf?*

- *Enjoying time for myself and my hobby doesn't mean I don't put my spouse first.*

- *I don't understand his quick reaction to others' needs but not to mine.*

- *How can he find so much to talk about with everyone else but not with me?*

- *I want his time to have fun to be with ME!!*

Loyalty has two essential components: *Faithfulness* and *Priority*.

Faithfulness: You Can Count on Me

Faithful is the term we reserve for those precious few we can count on to be truthful, trustworthy, and steadfastly committed to us—and few they are. "Many will say they are loyal friends," Proverbs 20:6 (NLT) says, "but who can find one who is truly reliable?" Faithfulness means being able to count on someone regardless of the issue and regardless of the circumstances. Faithfulness is what we vow first and foremost on our wedding day.

Priority: We Put Each Other First

Priority is something else we vow on our wedding day, though we may not have used that exact word. Priority is what we mean by the phrase "forsaking all others." To "forsake" means "to give up something *formerly held dear.*" The implication is to move someone new into first place in one's life. In the case of marriage, it means to put someone in her *rightful* place. The book of Genesis describes a process for the formation of a marriage relationship: "For this reason a man shall leave his father and his mother, and be joined to his wife; and they shall become one flesh" (Genesis 2:24). For a *Loyal* marriage relationship to be formed, there must be a cutting of ties and a shifting of priorities.

> **INSIGHT**
>
> I value the friend who for me finds time on his calendar, but I cherish the friend who for me does not consult his calendar.
>
> —*Robert Brault*

A man lies dying at home on his bed. Suddenly, he awakens! Drifting up the stairs comes the aroma of his favorite of all foods, his wife's special chocolate chip cookies. He drags himself from his bed and down the hallway. He stumbles down the stairs, pulls himself to his feet, and staggers into the kitchen. There on the kitchen table ... can it be? Yes! *Dozens* of thick, golden-brown cookies! He lurches toward the table and reaches out a trembling arm. .... Suddenly, a spatula smacks him on the back of the hand.

"Get away from those!" his wife snaps. "They're for the funeral!"

We all need to know that the marriage will come before the in-laws, the best friends, the children—even the funeral. We need to know that we are our mate's *Priority*.

Each of us is born with an instinctive "me first" attitude. But in marriage, the husband and wife have to cultivate a *"we* first" mentality—and each needs to know that his or her partner shares that value. Family therapist Terry Hargrave calls this concept "us-ness." "Instead of pursuing self-fulfillment," he writes, "the partners could dedicate themselves to caring for a third entity: their precious and vulnerable relationship."[1] Hargrave recommends that we think of marriage as a three-party arrangement. There's you, there's me, and there's *us*—and *us* comes first.

Amplifying Factors

The most devastating breaches of Loyalty are ones that involve basic marital fidelity. When we speak of a spouse being *unfaithful,* we mean only one thing. Each of us desires our spouse to be faithful in the most basic sense, but the dream of Loyalty goes much deeper. Unseen aspects of Faithfulness and Priority cause conflict in day-to-day married life.

She: *Where have you been?*

He: *At the hardware store. Why?*

She: *All this time? You've been gone for three hours.*

He: *Sometimes I just like to look around.*

She: *What in the world can you look at for three hours?*

He: *I don't know. What do you look at in the mall for three hours?*

She: *Did you stop anywhere else?*

He: *What's with the third degree? I don't have to report to you every time I go out, you know.*

Those who especially value Loyalty are sometimes vulnerable to doubt and thoughts of suspicion. This husband feels like he's being accused of something. *All this time? You've been gone for three hours.*

His wife's desire for Faithfulness and Priority may be amplified by the stories she constantly hears about husbands who are somewhat *less* than faithful. Her best friend's husband asked for a divorce last week, and the woman never saw it coming—she had *no idea.* If that can happen to her best friend, why can't it happen to her?

This wife dreams of Loyalty in a faithless world, and she longs for Priority in a world where wives are often *not* the Priority they should be. Even if her husband is a perfectly loyal man, he may still suffer from guilt by association—or at least *suspicion*. It isn't that she doesn't trust *him*; it's just that their marriage is surrounded by so much disloyalty.

He thinks his wife doesn't trust him. He's partly right; this *is* an issue of trust, but it's not entirely about him. Sometimes Loyalty arguments are about the world around you—and it's hard not to take it personally.

He: *Don't forget, Mom is coming over for lunch today.*

She: *Does your mother have to come over for lunch every Sunday?*

He: *Here we go on my mother again ...*

She: *It seems like every time we have a spare moment you're inviting your mother over.*

He: *She lives alone; you know that. She doesn't have anyone else.*

She: *She has your brother and sister. She's their mother too. Why don't they invite her over once in a while?*

He: *Why don't you like my mother? She's always nice to you.*

Marital researchers tell us that in-laws are one of the most common topics of conflict for married couples. Not necessarily. In-laws are certainly one of the most common *apparent* topics of conflict, but the real dispute is often over something deeper.

The husband and wife in our scenario seem to be having a classic in-law argument. They are indeed—but in-law arguments are often not about moms and dads but about Loyalty. The wife may actually *love* her mother-in-law, but she resents the *Priority* Mom seems to have in their marriage. The husband assumes that his wife must not *like* his mother. Why else would Mom be unwelcome? As the scenario ends, he is preparing to make the case that his mother is likable, and that she deserves to be liked—an argument that will go nowhere, because the disagreement was never about Mom's character in the first place.

The conflict isn't about whether Mom should come over but whether

Mom should come *first. It seems like every time we have a spare moment you're inviting your mother over.* She wonders, *Why isn't the same level of initiative and interest being shown in our marriage? First leave, then cleave; sometimes it seems like he never left. Whose side is he on, anyway?*

Dreaming of Shared Priorities

The Loyalty conflict is often about Priority, and it surfaces anytime something else seems to have claimed the attention and desire that you feel *you* rightly deserve, whether that something is a job, a hobby, an Internet site, another person—even your own children.

> *She:* I can't believe that in just five years Sarah will go away to college.
> *He:* I'm kind of looking forward to it.
> *She:* Looking forward to it! Are you kidding?
> *He:* I'll miss her, of course. But think of all the things **we'll** be able to do . . .
> *She:* You, maybe, but what about me? The kids have been my whole life!
> *He:* Thanks a **lot**.

He loves the kids—and he's glad that she loves them too. But when he hears the longing in her voice, he wonders if she feels anything remotely similar for him. It's been a problem for them since their first daughter was born. The wife seemed to love the newborn with an intensity her husband had never experienced himself, and at times he felt twinges of jealousy. When the baby first arrived, he expected his wife's love to expand to *include* the baby; instead, it sometimes seemed as if her love for him had transferred *to* the baby.

It's silly, he tells himself, to be jealous of his own children. He tries to remind himself how lucky he is to be married to a woman who is such a devoted mom—but it doesn't always help. Sometimes he finds himself pulling back from the kids, not because he doesn't love them but because he resents the Priority they've assumed. *It's always about the kids.* We need to love many people in our lives, but in marriage a person instinctively feels that he deserves a unique place in his mate's heart.

He feels ignored, and he longs to once again become his wife's Priority. But perhaps the reason that his wife has shifted her Priority to the children is that *his* Priorities have wandered as well . . .

The Word

Many will say they are loyal friends, but who can find one who is truly reliable?

PROVERBS 20:6 NLT

He: *I have to work late again tonight.*

She: *Again? That's the third night this week.*

He: *I can't help it; performance reviews are coming up.*

She: *Last week it was the big audit to get ready for; this week it's perfor-mance reviews. It's always something.*

He: *What do you want me to do, quit my job?*

She: *Of course not. I just wish you gave your family the same amount of attention you give your job. Even when you're here, your mind is on some project.*

He: *Why do you think I work as hard as I do? I'm not doing this just for me, you know.*

One of the most difficult balances of life is the tension between work and family. How much time do you spend at the office, and when is it time to come home? Spouses don't always answer these questions the same way, and the resulting argument is often about Loyalty.

Ironically, what one partner sees as an act of Faithfulness, the other may see as a lack of Priority.

She understands the demands of his job, and she actu-ally appreciates his dedication. She admires his position and his desire to provide for his family, but she still finds herself pulling back from him, afraid that her attempts to connect with him will be met with a dull "uh-huh" or a blank stare.

Part of the problem is that he never comes home at all—at least, not all of him. She would like him to be home more, but more importantly, when he is home she wants him to be *all there*—not just physically but in mind and spirit too. When she tries to explain this, he reacts defensively, suggesting that her demands are extreme and unreasonable. *What do you want me to do, quit my job?*

She feels misunderstood and taken for granted. Because he has withdrawn from the kids and no longer seeks to enter their world, she believes she must pull double duty. His lack of initiative in the fam-ily lowers her respect for him. She decides that she won't ask for his involvement anymore; she'll simply leave him alone and take care of the family's needs on her own.

If they continue this way, she may never know that he really wants to be a vital part of her world. And sadly, he may never understand that she longs for him to be the hub of the family and have the sense of Priority he desires. It may all be lost in the whirlwind of conflicting desires over Faithfulness and Priority.

> *She:* *Do you think she's pretty?*
>
> *He:* *Who?*
>
> *She:* *You know who.* **Her.**
>
> *He:* *Her? I didn't notice.*
>
> *She:* *You noticed. I can tell when you look at another woman, Ted.*
>
> *He:* *Okay, so I look sometimes. But I don't touch.*
>
> *She:* *Oh,* **that's** *a big comfort.*
>
> *He:* *Look, I'm only human. You expect too much, you know that?*

Husbands sometimes allow their eyes to wander—and wives notice when they do. "I still don't understand why he looks at other women," one wife lamented on our survey. Husbands tend to view an occasional visual tryst as a harmless indiscretion, but wives often see it as something more—as a kind of visual *unfaithfulness.* "You have heard that it was said, 'Do not commit adultery,'" Jesus once said. "But I tell you that anyone who looks at a woman lustfully has already committed adultery with her in his heart" (Matthew 5:27–28 NIV). Loyalty begins in the heart and works outward. True Faithfulness, in other words, is revealed in small things. As Jesus reminded us on another occasion, "Unless you are faithful in small matters, you won't be faithful in large ones" (Luke 16:10 NLT).

"One thing that gets people through difficult spots is fidelity," author Michael Leach writes, "not just fidelity to sexuality, but to the other person's emotions, to compassion, to kindness. Those who value fidelity can get through anything."[2] Those who value Loyalty long to know that their mate is *consistently* faithful, in attitude as well as in action, in public as well as in private, in small matters as well as in large.

She: Boy, this restaurant is expensive.

He: Don't worry about it. I'll put it on my expense account.

She: How can you do that? This isn't a business meeting.

He: I just got back from a business trip, remember? They don't know exactly when I returned, so I just tack it on to the end of the trip. Presto! A free meal.

She: Wouldn't they fire you if they found out?

He: Who's going to find out? I do this all the time.

She: You do? But isn't that . . . dishonest?

He: Look, I thought you might like to go to a nice place for a change. We can still go to Burger King, you know.

INSIGHT

**We laugh at honor
and are shocked
to find traitors in
our midst.**

—C. S. *Lewis*

When Teddy Roosevelt was a young man, he worked as the foreman of a cattle ranch in Colorado. One day one of the ranch hands came to Roosevelt and told him that a stretch of wire had broken down, and several unbranded cattle from the neighboring ranch had wandered through onto their land. "I branded them and mixed them in with our own herd," the man said with a wink.

"Get your gear and get out," Roosevelt said. "You're fired."

The news of the ranch hand's immediate dismissal surprised everyone. After all, hadn't the man acted in his employer's best interests? Isn't that Loyalty? And besides, would the neighboring ranch have even missed a few wandering cattle? Asked about his decision, Roosevelt replied, "A man who will steal *for* me is a man who will steal *from* me."

Roosevelt understood that true Loyalty has no boundaries. A man who is dishonest at work will be dishonest at home. A woman who will talk to you about other people will talk to other people about you. A man who will steal *for* you is a man who will steal *period.*

That's why it's hard to trust the Loyalty of someone who seems to be faithful to nothing or no one else. If you're not loyal to others, can I really be confident that you're faithful to me? Why are you making an exception in my case?

Now it's time to consider how the dream of Loyalty relates to *your* marriage. Consider the following questions and ask whether each of them is true of you always, sometimes, or never.

"*Of course I'd like to know how you've been feeling lately. Why don't you Facebook me?*"

LOYALTY INVENTORY—Faithfulness	Always	Sometimes	Never
Do I betray my mate's confidence by the way I talk about him when he's not present?			
Do I joke about my mate in the presence of other people and later find out she is angry about what I said?			
Do I look at the opposite sex in a way that shows interest?			
Does my mate ever express disappointment about the way I notice the opposite sex?			
Could my mate walk in on me in any circumstance without me being uncomfortable?			
Does my mate ever have doubts about my faithfulness?			
Do I confide in my mate above anyone else about my personal issues and concerns?			

LOYALTY INVENTORY—Priority	Always	Sometimes	Never
Do I find myself having a difficult time saying no to others because their needs seem significant or urgent?			
Does my mate ever voice displeasure with the amount of time I spend with people outside our home?			
Do I sometimes put the needs of my children before the needs of my spouse?			
Does my mate ever voice a feeling of neglect when it comes to his place in our marriage?			
Do I put as much thinking and creativity into my marriage as I do into my work or hobbies?			
Does my mate ever voice regret about being taken for granted?			
Do we have things that we enjoy doing together or talking about other than jobs, children, or the business of running the home?			

Finding the Root

On a scale from one to ten, how important is Loyalty to you? Place an X where you think you belong. Now put an O where you think your mate belongs.

1   **10**

The Word
Faithful are the wounds of a friend, but deceitful are the kisses of an enemy.

PROVERBS 27:6

Are there recurring arguments in your marriage that you think might be driven by the desire for Loyalty? What are they about?

Do you think there is something from your past that makes your desire for Loyalty especially important to you? Have you ever discussed this with your mate?

Do you think there is something happening in your life right now that could be heightening your desire for Loyalty?

Dreaming Together: Loyalty

There's no greater virtue than Loyalty, but even Loyalty has a dark side when it's taken to extremes.

THE GOOD SIDE OF LOYALTY	THE DARK SIDE OF LOYALTY
Faithful to a fault	Overlooking serious faults
Devoted to your mate	Idolizing your mate
Making your mate your priority	Ignoring all other priorities
Wanting your mate to be faithful	Jealous and suspicious
Wanting to be your mate's priority	Selfish and demanding

A Tip for Spouses of the Loyalty-Minded

If Loyalty is a bigger concern for your mate than it is for you, how can you begin to satisfy his desires for Faithfulness and Priority? A helpful way to demonstrate Loyalty to your mate is by *making a habit of offering accountability.*

As our children were growing up, we tried to impress upon them the difference between *trust* and *accountability.* We told them that we would always take them at their word. If our son said he would be at Todd's house, we trusted that that is where he would be. But if he left Todd's house to go to David's house instead, we asked him to call us and let us know of his change in plans. Our motive wasn't to constantly keep tabs on him or to track his every move. We didn't *distrust* him; it's just that there was always a chance that we might need to get in touch with him, and so we needed to know his whereabouts. It wasn't an issue of *trust;* it was an issue of accountability.

Instead of allowing your Loyalty-minded wife to struggle with vain imaginations, you can help fulfill her desires for Loyalty by *making a habit of offering accountability.* Instead of waiting for her to ask where you've been or why you were gone so long, tell her in advance. If you're going to be late getting home, call first. If you have to make a stop on

INSIGHT

Always do what you say you are going to do. It is the glue and fiber that binds successful relationships.

—*Jeffry A. Timmons*

the way home, let her know. If an errand takes much longer than you expected, tell her why *before* she asks. By making a habit of doing these simple things, you are *offering accountability*. You are saying to her, "I have nothing to hide, and I have nothing to be ashamed of. I will live my life before you as an open book." Remember, *offering accountability* is the key. If she has to request it, it only feeds her imagination: "Why do I have to ask for this? What does he have to hide?"

We can offer accountability in other areas too. Tell your mate she's free to read your e-mail or check your Internet history. If you receive a personal letter, ask him if he'd like to see it. If she walks in just as you hang up the phone, tell her who you were talking to—don't wait for her to ask. Make a habit of *offering* accountability, and trust may be less of an issue in the future.

Another simple but powerful way to *offer accountability* is to remind your mate of your faithfulness. From time to time, look your Loyalty-minded mate in the eye and say, "I just want you to know that there is no one else. I am completely faithful to you, and I love only you." If this sounds to you like stating the obvious, that's probably because Loyalty is not your issue. Your Loyalty-minded mate *wants* to trust you, and you can help relieve those nameless fears and nagging doubts by simply reminding her of your love and commitment.

Let's apply the principle of *offering accountability* to a scenario we saw earlier in this chapter . . .

> *She:* *Where have you been?*
> *He:* *At the hardware store. Why?*
> *She:* *All this time? You've been gone for three hours.*

He was gone longer than she expected, and a Loyalty conflict is under way. But if he had applied the principle of *offering accountability*, the conversation might have taken a much different turn.

> *She:* *Where have you been?*
> *He:* *At the hardware store. I know I was gone longer than I said I'd be, but I got to looking at power tools, and I started reading some of the*

instruction manuals. I stopped for gas, and then I came straight home. Sorry if you were worried about me—I'll try to call next time.

It was a simple thing, but by showing a willingness to reveal his whereabouts—by *offering* accountability—he protected his Loyalty-minded wife from doubt and suspicion.

A Tip for the Loyalty-Minded

If Faithfulness and Priority *are* especially important to you, what can you do to avoid the extremes of jealousy, possessiveness, or suspicion? A helpful first step is to begin to *voice gratitude and appreciation for faithfulness.*

As we said earlier in this chapter, those who especially value Loyalty are sometimes vulnerable to doubt and thoughts of suspicion. You can help resist the temptation of suspicion by reminding yourself of your mate's track record of faithfulness—and even more important, by thanking him for it.

First Thessalonians 5:18 (NIV) tells us to "give thanks in all circumstances"—not to merely *feel* gratitude but to *express* it. Something about thanksgiving transforms doubt and reinforces hope. Remember, suspicion grows best in a vacuum—wherever there is an absence of knowledge or encouragement. By giving thanks, we constantly fill the vacuum of doubt with reminders of past Loyalty.

And don't forget, thanksgiving has a transforming effect on both the giver *and* the receiver. By expressing gratitude to your mate for his Faithfulness and Priority, you make it much easier for him to hear your occasional doubts. As more than one man commented on our survey, "I need to hear what I'm doing *right* before I can hear what I'm doing *wrong.*"

Let's return to our scenario again. Instead of raising concerns about Loyalty, what if the wife had instead tried to *voice gratitude and appreciation for faithfulness*? How could things have gone differently?

She: Where have you been?
He: At the hardware store. Why?

She: *Look, I don't mean to doubt you. One of the things I appreciate most about you is your faithfulness. I've always been able to trust you, and I can't tell you how important that is to me. It's just that these thoughts cross my mind sometimes . . .*

He: *I'm sorry I was gone so long. I'll call next time.*

Security

Loyalty

RESPONSIBILITY

Caring

Order

Openness

Connection

THE DIFFERENCES THAT DIVIDE

"That is not a fashion statement. That is a fashion obscenity."

3 RESPONSIBILITY:
OBLIGATION and EXPECTATION

Joy: Tim and I once took a test called the Keirsey Temperament Sorter to help us understand our different personalities. Each of us had to fill out a seventy-question survey.

Tim: Which was more than my personality wanted to do in the first place.

Joy: Our answers were evaluated, and we were told that we each had a basic temperament type—a different temperament type—and that this temperament type predicted what we would do and say in different situations. My type was called "the most sociable of all types."

Tim: While mine was called "incurable, but at least not contagious." At least, that's what Joy called it.

Joy: We were each given an article that described our temperament type in detail. Mine said, "This temperament type has a well-developed sense of tradition [and] takes the 'rights and wrongs' of the culture seriously." People with this temperament type often feel a strong sense of obligation and responsibility.

Tim: On the other hand, I was described this way: "Authority derived from office, position, or wide acceptance does not impress this temperament type. Only statements that are logical and coherent carry weight. External authority per se is irrelevant." People with this temperament can seem individualistic and even arrogant.

Joy: You can imagine some of the conversations we've had.

Tim: Needless to say, Joy and I have a very different natural sense of Responsibility. I wish I had a dollar for every time we've had a conversation like this . . .

Joy: "Are you going to wear those pants?"

Tim: "What's wrong with them?"

Joy: "They're white. You're not supposed to wear bright white pants in the winter."

Tim: "Who made up that rule?"

Joy: "Everybody knows that."

Tim: "I don't know that."

Joy: "This from a man who would wear tennis shoes to a wedding."

Tim: (A long pause) "And your point would be?"

Joy: "I don't make up these rules. You're just not supposed to wear bright white in the winter, that's all."

Tim: "So someone I never met makes up a rule that makes no sense, and I'm supposed to follow it?"

Joy: "Why don't you wear your underwear outside your pants while you're at it?"

Tim: And that's about as far as the conversation gets. The problem is, Joy often feels a sense of Responsibility where I feel none. And that, as this chapter describes, often leads to conflict.

Joy: Where did you get that shirt?

Should, Ought, and Must

The *Responsibility* conflict begins with the word *ought*—we *ought* to do this, we *ought* to take care of that. In marriage, one partner often has a greater sense of duty to follow the dictates of laws, customs, fashions, and the expectations of others. These are the rules—we *ought* to consider them. Here are some comments from our survey that suggest the dream of Responsibility . . .

- *I care about how people see me and what they think about us.*

- *I wish she would lighten up and not major on the minors.*

- *Why is she so fussy about traffic laws?*

- *We repeatedly disagree over child rearing. What are the rules?*

- *We disagree about legalism vs. Christianity.*

- *He doesn't see the need to maintain and improve our home and allows it to go downhill.*

- *I don't understand her "black-and-white" approach to life.*

- *We disagree about getting bills paid on time.*

Laws are carefully defined, but customs, fashions, and the expectations of others are more ambiguous, and that's what leads to the Responsibility conflict. In marriage, most disagreements don't arise from what's said but from what's left unsaid—from what's *assumed*—and two different people can have very different assumptions about what *ought* to be done. There are two components of the value of Responsibility: *Obligation* and *Expectation*.

Obligation: What One Owes

Obligation is an internal sense of what is *owed*. Every culture has thousands of unwritten customs and mores that everyone has to learn in order to fit in: It's not polite to stare, the fork goes on the left, never shout in church, and always use a tissue (not your sleeve). These are all things we're told we *ought* to do, but each of us has a different sense of just how important it really is to comply. After all, exactly whom are we obeying, and why? Where do these rules and regulations come from? Why were they created? Are they still relevant? Are they reasonable and practical? No one knows the answers, but still that inner feeling of *oughtness* persists. That's what we call Obligation.

Expectation: What Others Require

Whereas Obligation is your sense of how important it is to comply, *Expectation* is your idea of what other people require of you. What do the neighbors expect of me? What do they think I should do? What is appropriate behavior, and when am I "out of line"? When am I in style, and when am I embarrassing myself—or my spouse? Expectation asks the question, "What will people think?"

Different People, Different Rules

To be fair, *all* of us are governed by some internal sense of Obligation and Expectation. No law prevents a man from wearing his underwear outside his pants—but with the exception of a few rock stars, no one does. There is a word for someone who rejects *all* of the Obligations and Expectations of a society: *sociopath*. We all operate within *some* unspoken guidelines of appropriateness and civility; we just don't always agree on what those guidelines are or how important it is that we obey them. This difference in internal value systems is what creates the Responsibility conflict.

> She: *Why are you eating your chicken with your fingers?*
>
> He: *Because it's barbecued chicken. You always eat barbecued chicken with your fingers.*
>
> She: *Not in a restaurant you don't.*
>
> He: *What difference does it make?*
>
> She: *It looks sloppy, for one thing.*
>
> He: *It doesn't seem sloppy to me; it seems practical.*
>
> She: *Plus, it makes you look immature.*
>
> He: *Look at that guy over there. See? He's using his fingers.*
>
> She: *He's eating ribs, not chicken.*
>
> He: *What's the difference?*
>
> She: *See that man over there? **He's** using a knife and fork.*

> **INSIGHT**
>
> A respectable person is one who conforms to custom. People are called good when they do as others do.
>
> —*Anatole France*

Responsibility conflicts can begin over the simplest rules—or two different *understandings* of the rules. As he sees it, *you always eat barbecued chicken with your fingers.* But to her, there's a proviso in this case: *not in a restaurant you don't.*

They begin to compare rule books: Barbecued chicken is in, baked chicken is out; ribs are in, chicken is out. They obviously disagree, so he asks if the rule is really important. The answer is obvious: To him it's not important at all, but to her it is. That's because she has the greater sense of Responsibility.

Now they begin to do two things that rarely work in a Responsibility conflict. First, she tries to convince him of the *reasonableness* of the rule: Eating chicken with your fingers makes you look both sloppy and immature. Not to him—to him it's a matter of simple convenience. So much for being reasonable.

Next, he appeals to the example of others. *That* guy doesn't recognize the rule, so why should I? She in turn searches for her own testimonial: *But that one over there is using a knife and fork.*

They may spend the next hour scouring the restaurant for supporters of their own perspective. Dinner may be over before they realize that they were never really arguing about chicken at all. They were arguing about Responsibility.

She: Why didn't you cut the grass this weekend?

He: I didn't have time. I was playing golf, remember?

She: Well, you'd better cut it after work today.

He: It can wait 'til next Saturday.

*She: You're going to leave it like that for a **week**? What will the neighbors think?*

He: Who cares what the neighbors think?

She: I care, and so should you.

He: What about the Gunthers next door? They've had that rusty old swing set in their backyard for years. It's an eyesore, but I don't complain about it.

She: I agree, but we can't tell them that.

He: If we can put up with their swing set, then they can put up with our grass.

She: You just don't care about anybody but yourself.

They both know the grass needs to be cut, but they differ as to why. To him, it needs to be cut for purely practical reasons, and so it can wait until another weekend. But to her, the grass needs to be cut for a much more urgent reason: The neighbors *expect* it to be cut.

At least *she* thinks they do. The neighbors have never said so, of course, nor are there any neighborhood covenants or bylaws about the acceptable length of Kentucky bluegrass. If there were, there would be no disagreement. The Responsibility conflict is about what *isn't* said.

He suggests that their neighbors have also failed to keep some of *their* obligations. *What about the Gunthers next door?* If the neighbors don't follow the rules, why should they? The argument doesn't satisfy her. After all, someone else's failure to act responsibly is no excuse for their *own* disobedience.

They finally arrive at a stalemate with a misunderstanding of the other person's dream. *She* thinks he's just plain selfish, while *he* thinks she cares too much about what other people think. This is how the Responsibility conflict usually ends.

> He: *Have you looked at the van lately? It's an unbelievable mess!*
> She: ***You*** *try driving four kids around all day.*
> He: *Why don't you clean it up?*
> She: *Why? So the kids can just trash it again?*
> He: *What are you saying—you're just going to leave it like that forever?*
> She: *I'm saying I just haven't gotten around to it.*
> He: *Well, you need to get around to it.*
> She: *What's the big deal?*
> He: *A car should never be allowed to get in that condition.*

This husband and wife would both like to have a clean car, but for different reasons, and so they come to the argument with a different sense of priority. For her, cleaning the van is a low priority. It would be *nice,* but all the other demands of raising and transporting four kids come first. She'll clean the car whenever she gets around to it.

But for him, cleaning the van is a much higher priority, because his desire is fueled by his sense of Responsibility. *A car should never be allowed to get in that condition.* Why? Who says so? If you pressed him, he would have a very difficult time answering those questions—at least to her satisfaction. Maybe he would be embarrassed if his friends saw the car. Not her; she thinks her friends should understand. Maybe his own mother always kept the family station wagon spotless, or maybe his father always complained that she didn't. Whatever the reason, he now has an inner sense of certainty that a car *ought* to be kept clean. He has a dream.

And to whom is this Obligation owed? To General Motors? To the neighbors, who never see the inside of their van? Again, he would have a difficult time answering. This is a debt owed to the car, to their family, and to the universe itself. This is not about someone else's requirement; this is an internal sense of Obligation. We *ought* to clean the car because . . . we just *ought* to.

> He: *You need to slow down here. See the sign? Thirty-five miles per hour.*
>
> She: *There's no way this should be a thirty-five zone. Fifty maybe, but not thirty-five.*
>
> He: *They must have had a good reason for making it thirty-five.*
>
> She: *What reason? There isn't a school within ten miles. It's a residential area, but there are no driveways that connect with this street.*
>
> He: *I don't know the reason. All I know is the sign says thirty-five.*
>
> She: *Well, I'm not going to spend the whole day on this street just because somebody put up a sign.*
>
> He: *You can't obey only the laws that make sense to you. What would happen if everybody did that?*
>
> She: *Maybe we wouldn't have so many traffic jams.*

He wants to "obey earthly authorities" because it's the right thing to do. *All I know is the sign says thirty-five.* She wants to drive a little faster because it's the practical thing to do. *I'm not going to spend the whole day on this street just because somebody put up a sign.* In Responsibility conflicts that's often the standoff: *principles vs. pragmatism.* Because he values Responsibility, he always seeks to act out of principle. His first question—sometimes his *only* question—is always, "What is the right thing to do?" After all, what else really matters?

She, on the other hand, always asks, "What is the *best* thing to do?" She doesn't mean best *in principle*—she means the easiest, most sensible, and most convenient. It isn't that she wants to deliberately disobey; it's just that she values something more than obedience—in this case, her time.

> **INSIGHT**
>
> A gentleman is a man who uses a butter knife when dining alone.
>
> —*W. F. Dettle*

She sees her husband as unnecessarily bound by petty restrictions. He sees his wife as stubborn and rebellious. They both agree that "35 mph" is a rule. To her it's an unreasonable rule that can be disregarded. To him it's still a rule, and it *ought* to be obeyed.

She: The Garzas are moving this Saturday.

He: Oh?

She: They're moving themselves, you know. We should offer to help.

He: Did they ask for our help?

She: You don't wait for people to ask. You offer to help.

He: The Garzas have lots of other neighbors who can help them move. Why are we always the ones who have to help out?

She: Look, we have to at least drop by and see if they need anything.

He: Why do we have to?

She: Because that's what neighbors are supposed to do, especially if they're Christians. What will they think if we don't even stop by?

He: They'll think we have things to do on a Saturday too.

This is a true Responsibility conflict, one that involves both Obligation and Expectation. The neighbors are moving—how will they respond? Obligation speaks first. *We should offer to help.* To her, there is a principle involved here: When a neighbor is in need, you *ought* to pitch in. It isn't a matter of convenience; it's simply the right thing to do.

But to him there are practical concerns here. This is a Saturday, after all, and there's a price for helping the Garzas. A day spent loading a truck is a day not fixing their own home or playing with the kids. How important is this? Is their assistance really necessary? *Did they ask for our help?*

To her, this question touches on a second Obligation. Her unwritten rule is that you ought to help out, and you don't wait to be asked. Perhaps her parents taught her this value, or perhaps she came by it on her own; either way, it's a firm conviction for her now—but not for him. His pragmatic response is that lots of people are available to help the Garzas. *Why are we always the ones who have to help out?*

Obligation is getting nowhere, so now Expectation joins the conversation. If the principle of neighbors-helping-neighbors means nothing to him, he should at least think about what the Garzas will expect. *What will they think if we don't even stop by?* But even the power of Expectation isn't enough to persuade him.

She thinks he's selfish and uncaring, and he thinks she doesn't have to come to the rescue of everyone in need. After she helps load the truck on Saturday, they may continue their discussion about Responsibility.

The Word
Respect what is right in
the sight of all men.
ROMANS 12:17

> *She:* *I've been thinking about your mom. After her last fall, I'm not sure she should live by herself anymore.*
>
> *He:* *What do you think we should do?*
>
> *She:* *She should come to live with us, of course.*
>
> *He:* *With us? You've got to be kidding!*
>
> *She:* *She's family. You take care of family. You can't just put her in some lonely nursing home.*
>
> *He:* *My mom would take a lot of care. Do you have any idea how hard that would be on our family?*
>
> *She:* *John, we don't have a choice. You always take care of family.*

Decisions about caring for aging parents are extremely difficult—but for her, there's no decision to make. *She should come to live with us, of course.* To her husband it's a serious dilemma, and he begins to remind her of the potential costs and difficulties of such a decision. *My mom would take a lot of care. Do you have any idea how hard that would be on our family?*

It's not that she's unaware of the potential costs. She isn't naive, and she knows that she may have to pay a great personal price for this decision. It's just that, to her, all potential costs and liabilities are overruled by a single, overpowering principle: *You always take care of family.*

The problem is, she has no way to communicate the power of that principle to her husband. She may try to explain it, or justify it, or passionately defend it, but if he doesn't *share* it, he will not feel its *power.*

When her husband questions her decision, she simply repeats the principle: *You always take care of family.* He cannot understand how she can make such a quick decision about a matter with so many far-reaching implications. To her, it all boils down to a single question: Will we be Responsible?

Do these situations sound familiar? Why not consider the following questions to see how the issue of Responsibility relates to *your* marriage . . .

*"You know I don't care what other people think.
I married you, didn't I?"*

RESPONSIBILITY INVENTORY—Obligation	YOU	MATE
Who pays more attention to social or political issues?		
Who is more conscientious about when the bills are due and paid?		
Who cares more about basic etiquette when it comes to manners and fashion?		
Who is quicker to think that you should help someone in need, whether a neighbor, a friend, or people around the world through a relief organization?		
Who is more likely to suggest that you volunteer for something at church because it's the right thing to do?		
Who feels more obligated to have someone over because you were previously invited to their home?		
Who in your marriage is the one who writes the thank-you notes?		

RESPONSIBILITY INVENTORY—Expectation	YOU	MATE
Who attends the office party even if it's the last place you'd like to be?		
Who feels more of an obligation to keep a commitment even though it becomes inconvenient?		
Who calls if he or she is going to be late or not able to come?		
Who feels more responsible to give money when asked to make a donation?		
Who will return messages and e-mail to people even if it's inconvenient?		
Who feels more strongly that your word is your bond?		
Who considers the opinions of others rather than pleasing only himself?		

Finding the Root

On a scale from one to ten, how important is Responsibility to you? Place an X where you think you belong. Now put an O where you think your mate belongs.

1   **10**

Are there recurring arguments in your marriage that you think might be driven by the desire for Responsibility? What are they about?

Do you think there is something from your past that makes your desire for Responsibility especially important to you? Have you ever discussed this with your mate?

Do you think there is something happening in your life right now that could be heightening your desire for Responsibility?

Dreaming Together: Responsibility

Some of us feel a strong desire to be Responsible. But what happens when a sense of Obligation and Expectation go too far?

THE **GOOD** SIDE OF RESPONSIBILITY	THE **DARK** SIDE OF RESPONSIBILITY
Valuing the opinions of others	Ruled by the opinions of others
Submitting to proper authority	Yielding to any authority
Principle-oriented	Rule-bound
Sense of right and wrong	Sees only black-and-white
Polite and mannerly	Formal and rigid
Fulfilling obligations	Acting only out of obligation

A Tip for the Responsibility-Minded

If you possess a strong sense of Obligation and Expectation, it's important to avoid the extreme of being completely *bound* by rules or the opinions of others. You can take a step away from that extreme by applying this principle: *Tell your mate what you want, not what he ought to do.*

Remember, the Responsibility conflict occurs when one partner feels a sense of Obligation or Expectation that the other does not. The solution is not to try to create the same sense of Responsibility in your partner—that may be impossible to do. The solution is to help your mate understand how important your sense of Obligation is to *you*.

Instead of telling our partners how we feel about their behavior, we sometimes make the tactical error of trying to convince them of the authority of our unwritten rule—but that only makes the problem worse.

INSIGHT

Rules are made for people who aren't willing to make up their own.

—*Chuck Yeager and Charles Leerhsen*

Instead of arguing about the reasonableness of the rule, or why it's important to obey, or listing friends and acquaintances who endorse the rule, a more useful approach is to simply *tell your mate what you want*. Even if your mate doesn't share your sense of Obligation or Expectation, he still has a desire to please *you*.

Let's go back to a scenario of a couple's conversation from earlier in this chapter. Their neighbors the Garzas are moving Saturday, and the wife thinks they *ought* to help.

She: *The Garzas are moving this Saturday.*

He: *Oh?*

She: *They're moving themselves, you know. We should offer to help.*

He: *Did they ask for our help?*

She: *You don't wait for people to ask. You offer to help.*

Now let's apply our principle: *Tell your mate what you want, not what he ought to do.*

She: *The Garzas are moving this Saturday.*

He: *Oh?*

She: *They're moving themselves, you know. We should offer to help.*

He: *Did they ask for our help?*

She: *I really want to offer to help. I think they expect us to, and even if they don't, I'll feel really embarrassed if we don't even offer. Would you please come with me on Saturday? It doesn't have to be all day—just a couple of hours.*

Even with this approach we can't guarantee that he'll jump at the opportunity to help. But we *can* guarantee that his wife will get a lot further than she would by arguing that her husband *ought* to help. Because his dream is not Responsibility, *ought* will not spur him to action—but his wife's feelings just might.

A Tip for Spouses of the Responsibility-Minded

If Obligation and Expectation mean more to your mate than to you, here's a first step to help you move toward her Responsible world. It's a derivative of the principle we just suggested to your mate: *Think about pleasing your mate, not obeying a rule.*

If you're not especially motivated by Obligation or a sense of what other people expect of you, what *does* motivate you? If you're like most people, you're motivated by a desire to please your mate. That's good—and that's the beginning of a solution to your Responsibility conflicts. Instead of endlessly debating whether you *should* or *shouldn't* do something, why not change your focus? Think about pleasing your mate instead of obeying a rule.

Think again about the Garzas and moving day. His wife believes they ought to help, but he feels no such Obligation, and now a Responsibility conflict is under way. But suppose he responded to his wife's sense of Obligation in a different way . . .

> *She: The Garzas are moving this Saturday.*
>
> *He: Oh?*
>
> *She: They're moving themselves, you know. We should offer to help.*
>
> *He: Did they ask for our help?*
>
> *She: You don't wait for people to ask. You offer to help.*
>
> *He: Wait a minute. You like to help out whenever someone is in need. We can't help everybody, so what I'd like to know is, how important is this to you?*
>
> *She: I know I tend to volunteer a lot, but the Garzas are our neighbors. I'll really feel embarrassed if we don't at least offer to help. This is very important to me.*

Once again, there's no guarantee that her husband will be lending a hand on moving day. But there's a much better chance, because this approach puts the request in completely different terms. Instead of asking himself, "*Should* I help?" he's now asking, "Am I willing to do what's very important to my wife?"

Security

Loyalty

Responsibilty

CARING

Order

Openness

Connection

"I don't know, let me ask him.
John, would you say you're an introvert?"

4 CARING:

AWARENESS and INITIATIVE

Joy: When Tim and I were first married, I thought it would be nice if he would call me from the office from time to time.

Tim: One day Joy asked me, "When you think of me during the day, why don't you call me?"

Joy: And he said, "Because I don't think of you."

Tim: That was a big win.

Joy: I thought as a newlywed I might have made a little more of an impression. I knew that Tim had a tendency to get lost in his work, but I guess I thought I might accidentally pop into his thoughts once in a while.

Tim: I did start calling you after that, remember?

Joy: That was very nice. But soon I realized that you had put a Post-It on your phone that said, "Call Joy." That's when I realized that you hadn't spontaneously started to think about me; you were just obeying a sign—like "Pay electric bill."

Tim: Isn't the important thing that I called?

Joy: I didn't need more phone calls. I just wanted to know that you cared.

Tim: In our marriage, Joy and I have had a lot of discussions about Caring. To put it bluntly, I will never care as much as Joy does about anything. Joy is a very Caring person. She cares about the kids, their friends, the teachers, the neighbors, even people on the other side of the planet. If Joy knows you, she cares about you.

Joy: Sometimes I wish I could care less, because it takes a lot of energy to care about everything. But I'm not sure how to turn it off. I do wish that I could mind-meld some of my Caring to Tim so I don't have to do it all myself.

Tim: I do care.

Joy: Yes, you do—but sometimes I have to ask you to.

Tim: By the way, how did you know about the Post-It on my phone?

Joy: I listen to your voice. I care.

Caring for Each Other

The word *Caring* literally means "feeling and exhibiting concern and empathy for others." The second chapter of Job tells us that when Job's three friends heard of his calamity, they "made an appointment together to come to sympathize with him and comfort him." Their first priority was to empathize, to feel what their friend felt—to Care. That's exactly what they did: "They sat down on the ground with him for seven days and seven nights with no one speaking a word to him, for they saw that his pain was very great" (Job 2:11b, 13). It's a great source of encouragement when people are willing to Care—and a common source of conflict when they're not.

Here are some comments from our survey that reveal underlying Caring disputes . . .

- *I still don't understand why I can do nothing and be in trouble the next time we get together.*

- *I need to be told more of the time that he loves me.*

- *I wish she wouldn't say "nothing" when I ask if something is bothering her.*

- *If I think something is important and he knows it, why doesn't he care enough to at least think about it?*

- *I don't want to be so "responsible" for the marriage and family. I want help.*

- *I don't understand what she needs from me to feel loved and cared for. I need concrete examples—like, "Here's what you're already doing; now this is what I want."*

- *I need him to "show" me rather than "tell" me that he loves me. I want cards, small gifts, etc., rather than the once- or twice-a-year large gifts.*

• *I don't understand why she tells others how much she loves me but has a hard time telling me.*

There are two components of Caring, and one flows from the other like a river from a stream. The stream is *Awareness,* and the river it produces is *Initiative.*

Awareness: Attentiveness to Your Mate

Awareness is mental and emotional alertness, an attitude of attentiveness to your mate's feelings and concerns. "Know well the condition of your flocks," Proverbs 27:23 warns us, and flock-watching is the primary activity of a Caring mate. We want our partners to notice little things, like when we're discouraged, or frustrated, or when we're sneezing our heads off—and we don't want to have to tell them. Flock-watching is exhausting when you have to do it alone, especially when those lambs begin to wander. We want our mate to Care enough to know how the sheep—and the shepherd—are doing.

> **INSIGHT**
> Casual neglect leads to catastrophic loss.
> —*Ken Gire in* Windows of the Soul

Initiative: Willingness to Engage

Initiative is what flows naturally from Awareness—at least it should. Initiative is the willingness to *engage* your mate about the problem. It's encouraging to know that your mate is at least conscious of your concern, but it means a lot more when he's also willing to *do* something about it. Awareness without Initiative is like faith without works—it is "dead, being by itself." In fact, Awareness without Initiative is sometimes worse than no Awareness at all. It's little comfort to know that your mate is aware of your burden but unwilling to lift a finger to help. In the reassuring words of Homer Simpson, "Just because I don't care, that doesn't mean I don't understand."

Caring Women

Most of the hidden issues we're describing in this book are not gender-specific. Loyalty and Responsibility issues, for example, belong to men and women alike. Caring is different; concerns about a lack of Caring are voiced far more often by women than men. As Susan Page writes, "Women's primary complaint about men is that they don't participate in the relationship enough. This objection takes many forms, but they boil down to the same root complaint: men are spaced out, preoccupied, not available."[1]

Women complain that their husbands are not aware and that they do not initiate—and this is the beginning of the Caring conflict.

> *She: I hate to have to ask this, but how do I look?*
>
> *He: You look great.*
>
> *She: Thanks a lot.*
>
> *He: I said you look great. What's wrong with that?*
>
> *She: What's wrong is that I have to ask you. Why don't you notice these things on your own? You don't notice because you don't care.*
>
> *He: I do care. And I do notice how you look—I just forget to say it.*
>
> *She: Really. So how do you like my hair?*
>
> *He: Your hair?*
>
> *She: I got it cut a week ago.*
>
> *He: Oh . . . it looks great.*

"How do I look?" a woman asks her husband. "You look great," he replies. As far as he knows, everything is fine. He responded to her simple question with a positive, enthusiastic response. He's unaware that a Caring conflict is already under way.

He missed the first part of her message: *I hate to have to ask this.* And she does—she hates the feeling that she has to *ask* for praise. It makes her feel small and selfish to have to say, "I'm dressed up today—did you notice?" She wonders why she always has to point out the obvious to him. *So how do you like my hair? I got it cut a week ago.* She offers a rationale for his lack of Awareness. *You don't notice because you don't care.* "I do care," he replies—he just doesn't notice. He can't be expected to notice every picky little thing that changes from day to day.

But his wife knows that he *does* notice picky little things. He notices home runs, new cars, and clever commercials on TV. He notices the things that he cares about—he just doesn't notice *her.*

The first step in Caring is simple Awareness. There will be no compliments or words of praise until he first begins to *notice.* As a friend of ours puts it, "If you were more *thinkful,* you might be more *thoughtful."*

> *She: I want to talk about the kids.*
> *He: What is it now?*
> *She: It's Jed. He's just so shy.*
> *He: He'll grow out of it.*
> *She: How do you know?*
> *He: I did.*
> *She: But he's not you.*
> *He: I wouldn't worry about it.*
> *She: You wouldn't worry about anything.*

In marriage, one partner often carries the *emotional* burden of the family much more than the other. Some of us approach life in a cognitive way; we take a logical, factual, arms-length approach to problems and trials. We think first and feel later—if we feel at all. We're able to compartmentalize problems and put them out of mind when we need to.

Others don't possess this facility. They are more emotionally oriented, and they feel the full emotional weight of every problem or concern. They long to release their burden, but the only way they can do so is by sharing it with someone else—someone who might not be thrilled at the prospect.

She's concerned about Jed. *He's just so shy.* She not only sees his problem, she *feels* it. She knows the awkwardness and isolation that shyness brings, and she worries that Jed's shyness is a possible indicator of an even larger problem down the road.

But her husband isn't concerned at all. *"He'll grow out of it,"* he reassures his wife, but his words offer little comfort. His words reveal less about Jed than they do about his own approach to problems in general: *I wouldn't worry about it.* It's true, and his wife knows it. *He wouldn't worry about **anything**.* Why does she have to be the only one who cares?

He thinks that shyness is a minor problem that will pass away with time, and he might be right. But he thinks there's no reason for concern, and that's where he has made his mistake. He needs to be concerned because his *wife* is concerned. Their discussion began about

Jed, but in a few minutes they'll be arguing about Caring.

> She: Can I talk to you about something?
>
> He: Sure.
>
> She: A month ago we talked about how the kids need to learn more about the Bible.
>
> He: Right. I remember.
>
> She: That's not really important to you, is it?
>
> He: What do you mean? Of course that's important to me.
>
> She: But you haven't done anything about it. I waited a month to mention it again.
>
> He: Well, things have been really busy. I've had a lot on my mind. But that doesn't mean I don't care about it.
>
> She: How can you say you **care** about it if you won't **do** anything about it? You do the things you care about.
>
> He: That's not true. I care about lots of things that I just can't get around to.

> **INSIGHT**
>
> We judge ourselves by what we feel capable of doing, while others judge us by what we have already done.
>
> —Henry Wadsworth Longfellow

A month ago she talked with her husband about a concern for the kids. "*Right*," he replies, "*I remember*." He hasn't forgotten, and he hasn't changed his mind—he just hasn't made any changes.

For an entire month she has waited for him to take the Initiative, but nothing has happened. She concludes that he must not care, because true Caring leads to action. *How can you say you care about it if you won't do anything about it?*

But he believes that Caring simply involves *concern*. *Of course that's important to me.* He's concerned about the problem, and that means he cares. He's right—Caring *does* involve concern, but true Caring doesn't stop there. Concern is just a form of Awareness, and Awareness has to be followed by Initiative.

As the disagreement progresses, he will argue that he *does* care because he's *concerned*, and she will argue that he *doesn't* care because he doesn't *act*. He thinks he cares because he is aware of the problem; to her, Awareness alone is not enough.

Caring Enough to Engage

Initiative doesn't always require major projects or Herculean efforts. Sometimes all it requires is a simple willingness to *engage*...

She: (Lets out a long sigh)
He: (Hears but ignores her, and continues to read his paper)
She: Boy...
He: You okay?
She: I'm fine.
He: (Returns to his paper)
She: (Another sigh)
He: You sure you're okay?
She: I guess so...
He: (Returns to his paper with increased intensity)

This is the beginning of one of the most common Caring arguments. In this stage, three things have become obvious to both of them: (1) Something is bothering her, (2) He is aware of it to some extent, and (3) He doesn't care enough to pursue it any further. He is about to learn the two mathematical principles that underlie most Caring conflicts: *Awareness + Initiative = Caring,* and *Awareness – Initiative = Conflict.*

Later in the evening, the Caring conflict moves to a more advanced stage...

He: You seem angry. Is something wrong?
She: Are you just noticing this now?
He: I asked you this afternoon how you were doing. You said you were fine.
She: I didn't want to interfere with your precious newspaper. How clueless can you get?
He: If something was bothering you, why didn't you say so?
She: A lot you care.
He: If I didn't care, why would I have asked?

That afternoon, something *was* bothering her—but now it's something quite different. Her discouragement rapidly evolved into a Caring conflict when her husband failed to care enough to engage her

---

The Word
In all labor there is profit, but mere talk leads only to poverty.

PROVERBS 14:23

about her burden. He doesn't understand that Caring is all about *Initiative*. He thinks he deserves credit just for asking. But she didn't want him to simply ask; she wanted him to *care*.

But he did ask, and she said she was fine. *If something was bothering you, why didn't you say so?* She didn't say so because he didn't really ask. To someone who appreciates Caring, "You okay?" is not a question at all—it's a throwaway line, like "Whassup?" or "Howzit going?" His question was just a cliché that indicated no real concern or eagerness to understand.

The husband in our scenario was Aware, but he did not Initiate—and so, in the eyes of his wife, he didn't really care.

> She: *What's the matter?*
>
> He: *I was playing golf with some new guys today. You should have seen their equipment—top-dollar stuff. And I've got these lousy, tarnished old golf clubs . . .*
>
> She: *Were you off your game?*
>
> He: *It's not that. I just kept looking at their equipment, and then back at mine. . . . You know, sometimes I feel like I'm ten years behind where I should be at my age.*
>
> She: *Try some chrome polish. That should shine them up.*

Communication is much more than the simple exchange of information. It also serves to reveal fears, express desires, and disclose secret longings. We communicate not only through our words but through the tone of our voice, the tightness of our jaw, and the tremor in our hand. Real communication sometimes takes place through "groanings too deep for words," and a Caring listener searches for the meaning *underneath* the message.

Something is bothering him. He isn't sure how to put it into words, so he begins with a comment about golf. *I've got these lousy, tarnished old golf clubs.* She assumes that this is an exchange of information, so she responds in kind. *Were you off your game?* It soon becomes clear that he is not concerned about golf clubs at all—clear, that is, but not to her.

Caring is the willingness to work through the complexity and confusion of someone else's emotions, something that the unCaring find

INSIGHT

People want to know how much you care before they care how much you know.

—*James F. Hind*

bothersome and draining. As a friend of ours expresses it, "I want a man who is strong enough to handle me when I'm a mess, and not just walk away when he doesn't know what to do."

It's easier to recommend a little chrome polish than to wade through the messiness of a midlife crisis. Maybe she was unaware, or maybe she failed to Initiate. In either case, from her husband's perspective she didn't *Care.*

> *She: I picked up your dry cleaning today.*
>
> *He: Good.*
>
> *She: And I took the Chevy in for an oil change. You said that needed to be done.*
>
> *He: It did.*
>
> *She: I picked up **your** dry cleaning and I took **your** car in so you wouldn't have to take care of it yourself.*
>
> *He: What do you want, a medal?*
>
> *She: A simple "thank-you" would be nice, instead of just grunting "good." You act like I owe you something. I do these things for you, you know.*
>
> *He: Did you ever stop to think how many things I do for you? I cut the grass and pay the bills and fix everything that breaks. Am I supposed to say "thank you" every time you do something around here?*
>
> *She: It wouldn't kill you once in a while.*

The most basic form of Initiative is simply expressing *appreciation.* In marriage, we perform a hundred daily acts of service for each other, and we usually do it without thought of recognition or reward. But from time to time we begin to feel taken for granted: Does he understand that I'm doing this for *him*?

The wife in our scenario points out a simple chore she performed on her husband's behalf: *I picked up your dry cleaning today.* She is saying, "I did a chore *for you*," but all he hears is, "I did a chore," and so his response is simply, *"Good."* But he missed the point of her message entirely. She was saying, "Are you *aware* that I did something for you today?"

She offers another example of her service, and once again he misses the underlying message. Finally, she's forced to come right out and make her point directly. *I picked up your dry cleaning and I took your car in so you wouldn't have to take care of it yourself.* Because he's joining the conversation late, he views her blunt request for recognition as arrogant and self-centered. *What do you want, a medal?*

In a healthy marriage, both husband and wife are motivated by a desire to please each other, and we want our mate to understand this motivation. *I do these things for you, you know.* We don't want a medal; we just want our efforts to be recognized. We want to be *appreciated.*

Over the course of years, the daily things we do for each other become so commonplace that we're no longer *aware* of them. At other times we *are* aware, but we take these acts of service for granted. We fail to express appreciation, and the result is often a Caring conflict. "You see all the things I do around here. Don't you *Care?*"

What role does Caring play in your marriage? Who puts the greater value on Awareness and Initiative? The following questions will help you decide . . .

> **INSIGHT**
> Words of comfort, skillfully administered, are the oldest therapy known to man.
> —*Louis Nizer*

CARING INVENTORY—Awareness	YOU	MATE
Who pays more attention to how a person "sounds" and the "body language" when someone else is speaking?		
Who asks, "What's wrong?" and genuinely wants the truth?		
Who is more aware of how the kids are doing emotionally?		
Who is the one other people come to when they are having a problem?		
Who will not want to discuss his hurts unless he feels that he is being genuinely cared about?		
Who seems to care deeply about others, even strangers he hears about on the news?		

CARING INVENTORY—Initiative	YOU	MATE
Who will try to meet a need before even being asked to help?		
Who takes the initiative in wanting to talk about the problems in your marriage?		
Who is usually the first one to suggest that something should be done about a problem or an injustice?		
Who will take the initiative to go to the school and talk to a teacher about a situation?		
Who takes more of the initiative in the area of intimacy and romance?		
Who needs appreciation because he often puts his own needs second?		
Who verbalizes more interest in your children's spiritual growth?		
Who is more willing to sacrifice time and money to help someone else?		

Finding the Root

On a scale from one to ten, how important is Caring to you? Place an X where you think you belong. Now put an O where you think your mate belongs.

1   **10**

Are there recurring arguments in your marriage that you think might be driven by the desire for Caring? What are they about?

Do you think there is something from your past that makes your desire for Caring especially important to you? Have you ever discussed this with your mate?

Do you think there is something from your past that makes Caring especially *difficult* for you? Have you ever discussed this with your mate?

Do you think there is something happening in your life right now that could be heightening your desire for Caring?

Dreaming Together: Caring

The world is a better place because of Caring people—but believe it or not, even Caring has a dark side when it's taken to extremes.

THE **GOOD** SIDE OF CARING	THE **DARK** SIDE OF CARING
Aware of the feelings of others	Vain imaginations
Shows appreciation	Shows appreciation to get appreciation
Cares even for strangers	Overextends at family's expense
Helps without being asked	Helps without being wanted
Puts her own needs second	Loses touch with her own needs
Cares how everyone is doing	Lacks healthy boundaries
Cares about details	Controlling or smothering

A Tip for Those Who Value Caring

If Awareness and Initiative come easily for you, and if you'd like more Caring from your mate, then do yourself a favor by *teaching your mate how to care*.

We want our partners to notice things on *their* own—we don't want to always have to *tell* them. Having to ask "How do I look?" takes all the satisfaction out of any compliment that might follow. So why should you have to *teach your mate how to care*? Doesn't that have exactly the same effect?

We're not advising that you tell your mate *what* to say—just *how* to say it. Caring conflicts begin when your partner fails to care, or when your partner doesn't express care *the way you want*. That's when it helps to explain to your mate what Caring looks like to you.

A man says to his wife, "That's a nice dress." He thinks that his comment shows Awareness, and by voicing his opinion he has taken the Initiative. If that's not Caring, what is? But from his wife's perspective, his expression of Caring leaves a lot to be desired. First of all, "nice" is an empty shell of a word—it means nothing at all. He might as well have said, "That dress is adequate." And second, his comment was not about her; it was about a *dress*. Would the dress have looked just as nice to him if it were hanging on a rack? It would have been much better to say, "*You* look beautiful *in* that dress." With just two minor adjustments, he would have had a real compliment there. Good advice—so why doesn't she tell him?

The reason we don't teach our mates how to care is that we tell ourselves we shouldn't have to. It's true, you shouldn't have to tell your husband to care—that's his responsibility—but you do have to tell him *how* to care if you want him to Initiate in the way that you most appreciate.

Remember the scenario from earlier in this chapter, where the wife had to ask her husband how she looked?

> *She: I hate to have to ask this, but how do I look?*
> *He: You look great.*
> *She: Thanks a lot.*
> *He: I said you look great. What's wrong with that?*
> *She: What's wrong is that I have to ask you.*

Now suppose she made the decision to *teach her mate how to care.* Her response might have been more like this:

> *She: I hate to have to ask this, but how do I look?*
> *He: You look great.*
> *She: I appreciate the compliment, but can I tell you something? If I have to ask you, your compliment doesn't really mean anything to me. I like it when you comment on specific things about my hair or my clothes or my body. That tells me you notice when I change things day to day.*

One quick lesson in Awareness and Initiative isn't going to turn him into Mr. Caring overnight, and there's still no telling when his next compliment will come, so don't give up if you have to remind him again. But chances are his next admiring comment will be a little more satisfying than "Nice dress."

A Tip for Spouses of the Caring

If you know that your mate places a high value on Caring, then you need to look for your own ways to demonstrate that you care. Remem-

---

The Word
Worry weighs a person down; an encouraging word cheers a person up.

PROVERBS 12:25 NLT

ber that Caring consists of Awareness and Initiative, so a first step in either area will be well received. We'd like to suggest a principle in the area of Initiative: *Make a practice of taking first steps.*

The word *initiate* means "to get things going by taking the first step." Those who value Caring are often burdened by the need to "get things going." They look at their homes, their children, their marriages, and they see a dozen areas where someone needs to just take the first step, and they feel that the duty always seems to fall to them. This is where our principle comes into play. To help relieve the burden from your Caring partner, *make a practice of taking first steps.*

Here's the secret that makes it all possible: To take the first step, you don't have to know what the second step is. The trick is to just get things rolling; it's easier to steer a moving car than a parked one. Once you get things going, you can figure out your next steps as you go.

Let's revisit another scenario from this chapter. Remember this one?

> *She:*   *Can I talk to you about something?*
> *He:*   *Sure.*
> *She:*   *A month ago we talked about how the kids need to learn more about the Bible.*
> *He:*   *Right. I remember.*
> *She:*   *That's not really important to you, is it?*
> *He:*   *What do you mean? Of course that's important to me.*

He *does* care—or so he says. But his Caring failed to impress his wife because his Awareness wasn't matched by Initiative. But suppose he's beginning to *make a practice of taking first steps.* In that case, the scenario might have gone more like this:

> *She:*   *Can I talk to you about something?*
> *He:*   *Sure.*
> *She:*   *A month ago we talked about how the kids need to learn more about the Bible.*
> *He:*   *I remember. The problem is, I don't know much about the Bible. So*

> **INSIGHT**
> Anything will give up its secrets if you love it enough.
> —*George Washington Carver*

here's what I did: I went down to that Christian bookstore, and they recommended this family devotional book. They said I could read a little of it each night at the dinner table, and then we could all talk about it. I thought that's how we could start.

She: That would be terrific!

His efforts may not sound like much, but to his wife it was *terrific*— because it's one area of life where she won't have to initiate. He's not exactly sure what his next step will be, but for now it doesn't matter. The important thing is that he's taken his first step toward real Caring.

Security

Loyalty

Responsibility

Caring

ORDER

Openness

Connection

"So I love the kids. Is that a crime?"

5 ORDER:

STRUCTURE and CONTROL

Tim: As you may have figured out by now, Joy and I take a different approach to a lot of things—including vacations.

Joy: Tim's idea of a vacation is to "head out on the highway, looking for adventure." He just wants to get in the car and go. To me, vacations don't work that way, especially when you have three kids.

Tim: Joy wants to plan things out in advance to make sure everything is taken care of and to make sure we get the most out of the vacation.

Joy: I want to make the most of the time because we're never sure when a time like this will come again.

Tim: For me, the very thing that makes free time free is the lack of Order. What I enjoy most is not knowing what the day will bring. I live under a schedule all week—who wants to do it again on vacation? The lack of planning is what makes the time enjoyable.

Joy: Which is great, but with four other people involved it's hard to just assume everyone will want to do what you want to do.

Tim: This difference in our approach to Order even extends to how we spend our spare time. When the kids were young, I would say to Joy, "We've got a couple of hours before dinner. Why don't you get out of the house for a while?"

Joy: And I would say, "Get out? Get out where?"

Tim: "Anywhere. Just go out and have fun."

Joy: "This kind of time is so rare—with no planning, I can't make the most of the time. If I just go, it won't be fun."

Tim: "Okay then, I'll be at Home Depot." I was offering Joy exactly what would satisfy me—a chunk of free, unstructured time. But that was precisely the kind of time she found frustrating. It took awhile before we realized that we had different attitudes about Order.

The Order of Our Lives

Some people like their ducks in a row. Others *own* ducks, but they're not exactly sure where they put them. Some prefer things organized, orderly, and predictable. They want things to go according to plan. They like to know where everything is, and they want to know what comes next. But others would rather take life as it comes. They prefer things spontaneous, unexpected, and unpredictable.

Life is comparatively simple for a just-married couple, but it grows increasingly complex as the years go by. With children, school, home maintenance, and a thousand other concerns to balance, Order becomes a critical issue and a source of great frustration—as some of the responses to our survey indicate:

- *I can't keep the house clean like he expects it. He thinks this is my lack of love and respect toward him because it is a priority to him.*

- *My husband has trouble with organization and leaves his things in piles in the dining room, office, etc.*

- *Why can't she be punctual? We are often late to things, and it causes stress to me because I want to be on time.*

- *We have differing standards of housekeeping. He wants the house "company clean" all the time, but we have six children.*

- *She forgets to update the checkbook.*

- *He says, "I'm going to have to get it back out tomorrow; why put it away tonight?"*

- *Why does she worry so much about things out of her control?*

Order conflicts involve fundamental differences in attitude. The argument may begin about finances, or personal records, or the way

INSIGHT

One of the advantages of being disorderly is that one is constantly making exciting discoveries.

—*A. A. Milne*

you spend your time, but it ultimately reduces to one of two underlying issues: the desire for *Structure* or the desire for *Control*.

Structure: A Plan for Everything

Structure is the dream of having a place for everything and everything in its place, but it's much more than that. The desire for Structure can extend not only to household organization but also to time, work, hobbies, shopping, leisure, and even sex. The underlying conviction is that *anything works better with a plan*. It's more efficient, more thorough, more purposeful, and a better use of resources—and therefore more enjoyable. Enjoyable, that is, if you happen to like Structure. For others, Structure is the very antithesis of enjoyment. How can you enjoy something that feels rigid, contrived, and predictable?

In chapter 1 we said that Security often requires you to limit your freedom in some way. Structure requires even more. Structure requires constant forethought, planning, and discipline. That's a high price to pay, but the price is well worth it to some, because Structure makes possible the second element of Order: *Control*.

> **INSIGHT**
> **Nothing is really lost. It's just where it doesn't belong.**
> —*Suzanne Mueller*

Control: Staying in Charge

Control is the desire to keep a firm grip on the steering wheel of life. We live in a world of unseen danger, financial setback, unexpected illness, and even random acts of terrorism. It's an uncertain world, and if you're not careful, the car can get away from you. How can you increase your chances of success and minimize your risk of setback or disaster? By maintaining *Control*. And what better way to maintain Control than through forethought, planning, and discipline? If things are in Order, they're under Control—at least the odds seem more in your favor.

Conflicts Over Order

Let's consider some common disagreements that can occur when ducks get out of line . . .

He: *I can't find your Visa receipts—again.*

She: *They're right over there.*

He: *Where?*

She: *On my desk. Look under that newspaper.*

He: *Your desk is a disaster! You need to keep this clean. You're supposed to put your Visa receipts in this box, remember?*

She: *Aren't they under the newspaper? See, here they are.*

He: *That's not the point. The point is, you're supposed to put them in the box.*

She: *The point isn't to find the receipts?*

He can't find her Visa receipts, and that not-so-subtle word "again" reminds her that it's not the first time. She organizes like an archaeologist, leaving receipts, papers, and unpaid bills buried in various geological strata throughout the house. "Out of sight, out of mind" is her motto, so she attempts to keep things accessible by laying everything out atop desks, end tables, dressers—on every flat surface in the house until there *is* no more space, and then she starts over again with more recent items on top.

Strangely, this system works for her. *Where are your Visa receipts? They're on my desk, under that newspaper.* If you need anything, just ask her—but you *will* have to ask her, because no one else can understand her mysterious system. So what? It's all the system she needs, so why do more? After all, *isn't the point to find the receipts?*

Not to him. To him, the point is to establish some kind of Structure. Even if her system works, it still drives him crazy because it's disorganized, haphazard, and undependable. They both want to find the Visa receipts, but he wants something more. He wants *Order.*

> **INSIGHT**
> Two dangers constantly threaten the world: order and disorder.
> —*Paul Valéry*

He: *What time is everyone supposed to get here?*

She: *I put "7:30 SHARP" on the invitations. You greet people at the door, and I'll get started on the refreshments.*

He: *Whatever.*

She: *We'll let them mingle until eight o'clock. Then we'll move people into the family room and start the game.*

He: What if people don't feel like playing a game?

She: They need to, because that's all I've got scheduled until 9:30.

He: For Pete's sake, can't we just relax and have fun?

There's nothing wrong with relaxing and having fun, but the woman in our scenario has difficulty doing both at the same time. Without a schedule there would be no Structure. She's in charge of the party, and a schedule is the best way to ensure that people have fun—or so she thinks. *They need to play a game, because that's all I've got scheduled until 9:30.* For those who value Structure, the best way to guarantee a good time is to schedule it in. For others, a party doesn't really get started until it gets out of Control.

Parties are common sources of Order conflicts, because one partner often bears more of the burden for planning and preparing the details of the event. Every party requires *some* Structure. You can't just throw open the doors and see who wanders in, and you'd rather not have strangers searching through your fridge for something to eat. There are invitations to send out, an apartment to clean, and hors d'oeuvres to prepare. If you're not the one who shoulders these responsibilities, it's easy to just sit back and "let the evening happen." But when you're the one in charge, it's happening to *you.*

We sometimes argue about our approach to leisure activities because time off together is so rare. We have to make the most of this opportunity; who knows when we'll get another chance? Both partners agree on this—but they *disagree* about exactly how to do it. For her, the best way to maximize the moment is through Structure and Control. But he lives with Structure and Control all week. For him, the very *absence* of Order is what distinguishes work from leisure.

They think they're arguing about who needs to plan ahead or who needs to relax and let his hair down, but they're really arguing about Order. The question they have to resolve is, "How much Structure does it take to have fun?"

He: Okay, what's the next item on the list?

She: We need a birthday present for your mom.

He: Check. Where do we look first?

She: I don't know . . . How about that gift shop over there?

He: Why that gift shop?

She: Why? Because it's right there.

He: Let's head to the mall first. When we get there we'll split up and hit the big department stores first. We'll each make a list of possible gift ideas, then we'll meet by the food court in half an hour to compare lists and decide where to go to make the final purchase.

She: I hate shopping with you.

Some people approach shopping the same way they would approach starting an online business—and why not? If you asked them, they would tell you the same elements are important to success in both endeavors: a clear mission, good market research, a specific timetable. The problem is, some people approach *everything* as if it were a business venture—and for the partner who doesn't favor Structure and Control, this approach is exhausting. *I hate shopping with you.*

She doesn't hate Order itself; she just hates to see it invoked unnecessarily. As we said before, Order requires *effort*—forethought, planning, and discipline. Do we really have to create an agenda just to buy a birthday gift?

For some people who love Order, the answer is yes. This is not just about buying a present; this is about conducting a successful shopping trip—one in which we are organized, aggressive, and thorough. Sure, we can buy a gift anywhere, but we can't find the *best* gift without Order.

The Time and Place for Order

We all know Order is necessary sometimes—but exactly when? When is Order desirable and helpful, and when does it just seem annoying and even compulsive? Sometimes conflicts about Order are also about *timing*.

Some would say that Structure and Control are *always* useful. Others would say, "For crying out loud, we're only *shopping*."

She: I'll be back in about three hours. You're sure you'll be okay with little Ben?

He: No problem. Have a good time.

She: *His favorite books are in a basket by his closet.*

He: *Check.*

She: *You could take him for a walk. It's a nice day.*

He: *Right. Whatever.*

She: *After his walk, he likes to . . .*

He: *Look, I'll take care of it. He's in good hands.*

She: *You're not planning to do any of those things, are you? You're just going to sit there and read the paper the whole time.*

He: *Are you leaving or not?*

Spouses sometimes accuse their partners of being *controlling*—an expression that often means, "You want more Structure than I do." The woman in our scenario offers her husband a series of suggestions for maximizing his time with little Ben, and she does so for two reasons. First, because that's the approach *she* would take with little Ben. She's a hands-on mom, and every day she looks for ways to increase her interaction with her son. She expects no more from her husband than what *she* is willing to give.

Second, she knows that Ben's time alone with his father is in short supply. She sees this as a rare opportunity for both of them, and the best way to maximize the experience is through Structure. *His favorite books are in a basket by his closet. You could take him for a walk . . .*

But her husband feels crowded and resentful. A less-Structured approach is what he was planning—or, more accurately, *not* planning. If Ben wants to play ball, they'll play ball. If Ben wants to read a book, they'll read a book. This is playtime, and he doesn't need a schedule to play with his own son.

Order conflicts are not always rooted in personality differences. You may desire Order in one situation and resent it in the next. Sometimes we just disagree about when Structure and Control are important.

She: *Did you get the new lawn mower put together?*

He: *It doesn't work. I'm taking it back.*

She: *What's wrong with it?*

He: *How should I know? I should have bought a better model. Look at all these extra parts that came with it.*

She: *Extra parts? Nick, did you read the directions before you put it together?*

He: *Of course not. Any idiot can put a lawn mower together.*

If Order is not your passion, there is no more annoying question than, "Did you read the directions?" *Of course not.* Directions are for fools, meant only for those who lack the insight and intuition to figure out a problem themselves. Assembling a product should be a spontaneous event—like *all* events—and the only necessary part of the directions is the cover, which shows an image of the finished product to get you headed in a general direction.

Those who work in customer service are frequently amazed by the aversion some people have to instruction manuals. They don't really hate instruction manuals—just instructions. They resent the idea of having to lay out all the necessary tools, and clear off an adequate and well-ventilated work space, and count all the wing nuts and clevis pins before they begin.

But lawn-mower manufacturers should not take this personally. These same people bake cookies without recipes, build gazebos without blueprints, and overhaul engines without consulting the repair manual. Needless to say, not all of these endeavors come out as well as planned—but then, they *weren't* planned. They were done for the sheer enjoyment of working freely without restriction or annoyance.

If you're the one who appreciates Order, it's hard to watch your partner build a gazebo that looks more like the kids' tree house, knowing all the time that a peek or two at the blueprint would have made all the difference. But just as you may dream of Order, your mate may value freedom and spontaneity with equal passion.

INSIGHT

Chance always favors the prepared mind.

—*Louis Pasteur*

He: *Honey, can I make a suggestion?*

She: *Sure.*

He: *Every time you put the rubber spatula away, you put it in a different drawer.*

She: *So? At least I put it away.*

The Word
An empty stable
stays clean, but no
income comes from
an empty stable.

PROVERBS 14:4 NLT

He: But I can never find it. Now, suppose we reorganize these drawers according to function. Cooking implements here, mixing implements here, and miscellaneous items here.

She: I don't want to have to memorize a filing system just to clean the kitchen!

He: But it's so simple, and it makes things so much more efficient.

She: I can always find the spatula—look, it's right here.

He: I make one suggestion and you have a cow.

She: I have a suggestion for you. Want to hear it?

A classic marital conflict occurs when a husband retires and suddenly brings his unharnessed creative energies to bear on his wife's household, sometimes resulting in the mysterious and untimely demise of the husband. He spent the last forty years as an accountant or an engineer or a systems analyst. He's been in her kitchen thousands of times before, but now, when he really *looks* at it for the first time, he sees dozens of confusing and inefficient systems that could benefit from his knowledge and expertise.

The problem, of course, is that she doesn't *want* his knowledge and expertise. His complaint is that he can't find the rubber spatula. So what? This is *her* kitchen, and she can find the rubber spatula whenever she wants it. This is *his* problem, but he sees it as hers. *Honey, can I make a suggestion?* She finds his suggestion obtrusive and even arrogant. He finds her response shortsighted and unappreciative. *But it's so simple, and it makes things so much more efficient.* But this is not about efficiency, this is about Order—*his* idea of Order.

In marriage, even though we "become one flesh," we still have private domains that belong to each of us. It's one thing for you to seek to Structure and Control *your* world, but it's another thing when you're seeking to Order mine. Nothing is easier to organize than someone else's life. We all leave nooks and crannies purposely unstructured, not because we dislike Order but because no one else's sense of Order seems to suit us. Sometimes the Order conflict is about whose *idea* of Order will rule.

Now it's time to consider the question of Order in relation to *your* relationship. How much do you value Structure and Control in your marriage? Respond to the following questions with *Always*, *Sometimes*, or *Never*.

"Do we have to do this every time you win an argument?"

ORDER INVENTORY—Structure	Always	Sometimes	Never
Do I prefer to keep a filing system with my papers organized in specific places (vs. having a general idea of where they are)?			
Do I put family photos in an album or in chronological order (vs. tossing them in a box or drawer)?			
Do I know the kids' schedules and plan ahead for upcoming events (vs. grabbing what I need as I go out the door)?			
Do I keep a running "to-do list" (vs. doing what I need to do as it unfolds)?			
Do I follow directions, recipes, or sewing patterns (vs. "winging it")?			
Is my garage neatly organized with tools and sports gear in designated places (vs. things just thrown into bins or boxes)?			
Do I make a list of what to pack and what needs to be done before a trip (vs. dumping the laundry baskets into the sunroof)?			
Do I enjoy watching home organization shows (vs. hyperventilating at the thought of them actually organizing yours)?			

ORDER INVENTORY—Control	Always	Sometimes	Never
Do I enjoy it when people drop by unannounced?			
Am I frustrated when someone interrupts my schedule?			
When I am in charge, am I more comfortable with a detailed plan?			
Would I prefer to be surprised by a special event (vs. being in on the planning)?			
Do I have a "hands-on approach" with my kids, knowing where they are and what they're doing most of the time (vs. a looser "I'm sure they're okay" approach)?			
Would I rather operate from a budget knowing exactly what I spend (vs. knowing I have enough, but not knowing exactly where it's gone)?			
Would I prefer to have some kind of structure on my days off?			

Finding the Root

On a scale from one to ten, how important is Order to you? Place an X where you think you belong. Now put an O where you think your mate belongs.

1   **10**

Are there recurring arguments in your marriage that you think might be driven by the desire for Order? What are they about?

Do you think there is something from your past that makes your desire for Order especially important to you? Have you ever discussed this with your mate?

Do you think there is something happening in your life right now that could be heightening your desire for Order?

Dreaming Together: Order

Structure and Control can help make Order out of chaos—but when Order goes too far, it creates a chaos of its own.

THE **GOOD** SIDE OF ORDER	THE **DARK** SIDE OF ORDER
Organized	Controlling
Efficient	Impersonal
Structured	Obsessive
Scheduled	Inflexible
Punctual	Impatient
Hands-on	Perfectionistic

A Tip for the Orderly

If Structure and Control are important values to you, you can effectively resist the tendency to become controlling or obsessive by *focusing on critical areas only.*

The problem with the dream of Order is that it can become all-encompassing. Order is not just the desire for a neater household; it's a way of looking at life—the view that *everything* works better with Structure and Control. It may be true that every area of your marriage and family could benefit from additional Order, but not every area is equally important. You can take a major step away from the world of the obsessive if you can distinguish areas where Order is *critical* from areas where it's merely *desirable.*

Earlier in this chapter we described a situation where an Orderly husband was searching with great frustration for his wife's Visa receipts. Their conversation went like this:

He: *I can't find your Visa receipts—again.*

She: *They're right over there.*

He: *Where?*

She: *On my desk. Look under that newspaper.*

He: *Your desk is a disaster! You need to keep this clean. You're supposed to put your Visa receipts in this box, remember?*

INSIGHT

Never claim as a right what you can ask as a favor.

—*John Churton Collins*

111

She finds the receipts, but her desk is a disaster. It's *always* a disaster, which drives his Ordered mind to distraction. This would be a good time for him to try out the principle of *focusing on critical areas only.*

He: *I can't find your Visa receipts—again.*

She: *They're right over there.*

He: *Where?*

She: *On my desk. Look under that newspaper.*

He: *You know, your desk is your business, but there are certain areas where we need to be better organized. I'm especially concerned about the credit card receipts—I need to go online and reconcile the bill at the end of the month. I'll make a deal with you: If you'll agree to put your credit card receipts in this box, you can do whatever you want with the rest of your desk. Deal?*

What does she have to lose? By *focusing on critical areas only,* he set up a crucial Structure while requiring only a minimal adjustment on her part. He moved toward her world without surrendering the critical part of his own.

> **INSIGHT**
> Establishing goals is all right if you don't let them deprive you of interesting detours.
> —*Doug Larson*

A Tip for the Less-than-Orderly

If your mate's desire for Structure and Control are threatening to drive you up the wall, one way to satisfy both her preference for Order and your desire for spontaneity is by *planning to be disorganized.*

As we said earlier in this chapter, we've often disagreed over our approaches to leisure time. One of us likes a schedule and a plan, and one of us likes to take things as they come. For years it seemed like a case of terminal gridlock—until it suddenly dawned on us that we could fulfill *both* of our desires by simply *planning to be disorganized.*

Now when free time comes along, we make a schedule—but within that schedule we allow times that are unstructured. We specifically schedule times that *have* no schedule, times when we will do whatever we want whenever we want to. By *planning to be disorganized,* we satisfy our desires for both Order and spontaneity.

The same principle applies to other situations as well. Earlier in this chapter we described a Structured husband and a spontaneous wife on a mission together to buy a birthday present . . .

> He: *Let's head to the mall first. When we get there we'll split up and hit the big department stores first. We'll each make a list of possible gift ideas, then we'll meet by the food court in half an hour to compare lists and decide where to go to make the final purchase.*
>
> She: *I hate shopping with you.*

If they had only *planned to be disorganized,* their excursion might have gone more like this:

> He: *Let's head to the mall first. When we get there we'll split up and . . .*
>
> She: *Hold it a minute. I hate shopping that way. Can we compromise? Let's do it like this: You can decide which stores we'll visit, and you can even decide the order of events. But once we get to the store, then we do it my way. No lists, no deadlines, no schedule —okay?*

It's not exactly what he wanted, but by *planning to be disorganized,* they managed to satisfy both of their desires—and they even managed to enjoy shopping in the process.

Security

Loyalty

Responsibility

Caring

Order

OPENNESS

Connection

"Okay, I get the point. I've got too much paper."

6 OPENNESS:

SOCIABILITY and ENERGY

Joy: If you haven't guessed it by now, I'm an extrovert. I'm what psychologists refer to as an "Open" personality.

Tim: While I, of course, am just the opposite. "Sorry—We're Closed."

Joy: Open personalities are often called extroverts. Extroverts like to be around people. We enjoy conversation and we feel recharged by relationships with others.

Tim: Introverts like people, too, but not so many and not all at once. We feel recharged by being alone, and conversation wears us out—especially conversation with strangers.

Joy: Tim has a button that says, "Go ahead and talk—I'll just be napping here."

Tim: And Joy has a sign on her door that reads, "Extrovert at work—Please interrupt me."

Joy: Tim has a clever way of letting his listener know if he's getting tired of the conversation. I learned this after about two days of marriage.

Tim: I turn my body away from the other person and I take one step away. Then I sort of rock back and forth a little bit . . .

Joy: It's his subtle way of saying, "This plane is going down and I'm bailing out."

Tim: It's actually very rude, and I try not to do it—but the temptation is always there. It takes energy to interact with people, and when you're an introvert, energy is always in short supply.

Joy: Open personalities are recharged by people, and closed personalities are exhausted by people.

Tim: You can imagine the difficulty we've had trying to come to agreement about friendships, parties, and social gatherings of every kind.

Joy: We've had to work hard to adjust to each other. There are still a
few things we need to improve, though . . .

Tim: Excuse me, this is where I bail out.

Balancing Sociability and Privacy

Openness has to do with your attitude toward people and your need
for privacy. Do groups of people invigorate you, or are your batteries
drained by social interaction? Do you prefer large social gatherings;
small, intimate groups; or no groups at all? Where do you instinctively
go when you need to *recharge*—do you seek the company of others, or
do you search for some space of your own?

Husbands and wives are sometimes very different when it comes to
Openness, as these comments from our survey illustrate . . .

- *My quietness is not a measure of my love for her.*

- *My need for individual time is not a rejection of him.*

- *I have a need for other women's friendships. It's okay to have an occasional cup of coffee without guilt.*

- *I need quiet time and alone time daily—not away from him, just time to be able to reflect and allow God to keep me balanced.*

- *She doesn't understand my lack of enthusiasm and energy at home—I gave everything I had at work.*

- *I don't understand his lack of need for relationships.*

We all desire some amount of intimacy and interaction with others,
while at the same time longing for some time to ourselves. In marriage,
everyone lives with this tension—but by nature, some of us want far
more interaction than others, and that's when Openness conflicts begin. Openness has two chief components: *Sociability* and *Energy.*

Sociability: The Desire for People

Sociability is the desire to be with other people, whether a single companion or an entire assembly. Far more than simply being "friendly"

or "outgoing," Sociability is an orientation that finds its greatest fulfillment through connection with others. Sociable personalities are traditionally referred to as *extroverts,* while their privacy-seeking counterparts are known as *introverts.* Whereas extroverts are Sociable, introverts are territorial—they seek private places both in the mind and in the world around them. Extroverts experience a sense of isolation when they're not in contact with others; introverts experience the very same sense of isolation when they're in a crowd. Extroverts enjoy parties, meetings, discussion groups, and neighborhood gatherings; introverts may prefer solitary activities, individual sports, or relaxing in front of the television.[1] Needless to say, Sociability can be a great source of conflict between differently oriented partners.

INSIGHT

There's one thing worse than being alone: wishing you were.

—Bob Steele

Energy: The Need to Recharge

Energy is the question of what drains you and, when those mental and emotional fuel cells are depleted, what recharges you once again. Extroverts tend to recharge in social gatherings; people are an energy source to them. An extrovert may be the last one to leave the party, and when it's over she may go looking for another because she is rejuvenated by the experience.

But introverts tend to recharge alone; people are an energy *drain* to them. An introvert may be reluctant to attend the party at all, and once he's there he may count the minutes until he can leave again. It's not that he doesn't *like* parties; it's just that parties wear him out. People require *Energy.*

Mates require Energy too. Different approaches to Openness can cause marriage partners to disagree about the amount of time they should spend together. An extroverted spouse may feel rejected by her privacy-seeking partner. But as communication scholar Julia Wood reminds us, "There is nothing wrong when we seek privacy; it doesn't mean a relationship is in trouble. It means only that we need both openness and closedness in our lives."[2]

There's nothing wrong with being an introvert *or* an extrovert.

However, extroverted husbands often marry introverted wives—and vice versa—and that's where the trouble begins. Imagine an introverted husband married to an extroverted wife. She values Sociability and draws Energy through interaction with others. Her husband, on the other hand, values privacy and prefers to recharge alone. They both return home after an exhausting day at work—how will they spend their evening?

In all likelihood, they will spend their evening arguing about Openness.

She: I'd sure like to see that new movie . . .

He: Why don't you go? It's showing at 7:30.

She: Will you go with me?

He: That movie doesn't interest me. I'd rather finish my novel.

She: It's only two hours.

He: No thanks. I'd rather read.

She: Never mind then. I can't go by myself.

He: Why can't you go by yourself? It's just a movie. Even if you go with someone else, you just sit there.

She: That's not the point. I can't enjoy a movie by myself.

He: I thought the point was to see a movie, not have a party.

Movie watching is a solitary activity—a roomful of strangers sitting side by side in individual seats, staring straight ahead at the screen without speaking a word. But a true extrovert will seek to turn even movie watching into a group event.

Because the woman in our scenario is an Open personality, two questions come to her mind simultaneously: "What movie will I see?" and "Who will I see it with?" To her, it's unthinkable that she would attend a movie alone. What's the fun in that? *I can't enjoy a movie by myself.*

But her introverted husband thinks the point in going to a movie is to see a movie, just as the point in going bowling is to knock down pins. To him, the most important question is always, "What will we *do*?" To her, the really important question is, "Who will we do it *with*?"

"Will you go with me?" she asks her husband, but the question he hears through his introvert's ears is, "Do you want to see this movie?"

"I'd rather read," he responds. Why would he want to see a movie he isn't interested in? To her the answer is obvious: "To be with *me.*"

He doesn't want to do an activity he isn't interested in, and she doesn't want to attend an activity alone. But there is one activity they do together—they both argue about Openness.

> *She 1: I think public schools give the kids much more exposure to different kinds of people.*
>
> *She 2: So do I, but it's hard to beat the quality of a private education. What do you think, honey?*
>
> *He: What?*
>
> *She 2: You weren't listening at all, were you?*
>
> *He: Were you talking to me?*
>
> *She 2: No, but we were talking, and you're sitting right here. You just tuned the whole thing out, didn't you?*
>
> *She 1: My husband does the same thing. It's like he has his own little private world, and when nothing I'm saying interests him, he just disappears into it.*
>
> *She 2: That's exactly what he does, and it drives me crazy because then I have to repeat everything.*
>
> *He: What?*

While Open personalities value Sociability, introverts are more territorial—and the private territory they withdraw to is sometimes in the mind. Introverts have an internal world, and the seclusion of this private sanctuary is never more than a mental step away. When there's nothing interesting going on in the real world, introverts simply retreat into a world of their own.

These two women are having a conversation—not a conversation *with* the man but a conversation right in front of him. But he's not interested in the topic, so he mentally checks out. When his wife finally asks him a direct question, they find his apartment vacated and his closet empty. *You weren't listening at all, were you?*

Extroverts have a hard time accepting this tendency or even understanding the capacity. How can you simply tune out a conversation that's going on right in front of you? To an extrovert, a conversation is a call to arms, an open invitation to participate. But an introvert doesn't want to expend his Energy on every fleeting exchange. The husband wants to know if this conversation involves *him*. *Were you talking to me?*

The introvert's approach to conversation is, "If you need me, call me." Otherwise, he'll be in a world of his own.

> He: *This should be a great party. I've really been looking forward to this.*
>
> She: *How long do we have to stay?*
>
> He: *How long do we have to stay? We haven't even got there yet! Why did you agree to come if you already can't wait to leave?*
>
> She: *I wanted to come. I just don't want to burn up the whole evening here.*
>
> He: *Burn up the whole evening? What are you in such a rush to get home to, the TV? Talk about burning up a whole evening!*
>
> She: *I don't know anybody there.*
>
> He: *That's the whole point of coming, to meet some new people.*
>
> She: *I'm just not up for meeting new people tonight.*
>
> He: *You're never up for meeting new people! You know, you are really getting dull.*

He's a party animal, and she's a party pooper. They haven't even arrived at the party yet and already she's planning her exit. *Why did you agree to come if you already can't wait to leave?* But she *did* want to come—she likes parties too. But being an introvert, she has begun to take a mental inventory of the Energy it will require to greet strangers, smile incessantly, and engage in dialogue for the next three hours straight.

He doesn't understand her attitude. He thinks her negativity sucks the life out of every get-together. She seems to drag her feet wherever they go. *You know, you are really getting dull.* It's hard to understand because, for him, parties are effortless. You don't have to do anything; you just show up—and you always feel better when you leave. But she thinks about parties the way she thinks about going to the gym. It's good for her, and she likes to go, but it's going to *cost* her.

I don't know anybody there, she complains. It takes less Energy to interact with an intimate group of familiar friends than to break new

121

ground with a roomful of perfect strangers. But to him, *that's the whole point of coming, to meet some new people.* Because he values Sociability, his boundaries are always expanding. For her, the path is narrow that leads to her door, and only a few at a time are welcomed in.

Neither one may enjoy the evening—not because the party was a flop but because they don't have the same approach to Openness.

> *She:* *There's a new Sunday school class starting up. I think we should join it.*
>
> *He:* *What's the topic?*
>
> *She:* *It would be a great way to get to know some of the other couples in the church. The main service is so large now, I hardly even recognize anyone.*
>
> *He:* *What would we be studying in this class?*
>
> *She:* *I don't know. It sounds like a good opportunity. What do you think? Do you want to go?*
>
> *He:* *How would I know? You don't even know what the class is about!*

Because she values Sociability, she instinctively evaluates an event in terms of its potential for interaction, and a Sunday school class would be just the thing. That's all she needs to know; her decision is made. *It sounds like a good opportunity,* she says to her husband. *Do you want to go?* But to him, it's a Sunday school *class,* and a class has to be about something. *What would we be studying in this class?*

Because he doesn't always think in terms of Sociability, he sees no *purpose* yet for the class. Without a clear purpose to consider, how does he decide to attend or not? *How would I know?*

He thinks she's impulsive, and she thinks he's antisocial. Our different views of Openness can cause us to approach the same event from completely different directions.

> *She:* *I saw an interesting book today. It's called* The Friendless American Male.
>
> *He:* *Oh?*

INSIGHT

The enthusiastic, to those who are not, are always something of a trial.

—Alban Goodier

She: I've been thinking . . . you really need some more friends.

He: Me? I've got all the friends I need.

She: Name one.

He: Well . . . there's Curt.

She: Curt? You call Curt a friend? You see him once every three months at a business convention. I'm not talking about casual acquaintances; I'm talking about real friends.

He: How about Sam? Sam's a friend.

She: Okay, so you've got one friend. But you need more than that.

He: Why?

She: Why? You don't understand why you need friends?

He: I don't understand why I need more friends. One is enough for me.

Everyone needs friends—but *how many* friends, and what *kind*? Our contrasting approaches to Openness cause us to answer those questions in very different ways.

She values Sociability, so she treasures friendship. She never has enough friends, and she's always eager to make a new one. Without her friends she would feel isolated, alienated, and disconnected.

She looks at her introverted husband and she sees a man who has no friends—a man who, therefore, must be isolated, alienated, and disconnected. Because she loves her husband, she wants to help. *You need some more friends,* she tells him, and she is dumbfounded by his reply: *I've got all the friends I need.*

How is that possible? No one has all the friends they need! She challenges him on the number and quality of his friendships. *I'm not talking about casual acquaintances; I'm talking about real friends.* Her friends meet regularly for coffee to discuss intimate details about life, love, and family. *His* friends meet once a year to compare hockey tickets. After careful cross-examination, the fact emerges that he has but one true friend. But somehow, that's enough for him.

She doesn't just want her husband to have more friends—she wants her husband to have *her* kind of friends—intimate companions who are numerous and near. She may think of her husband as disconnected, but he just approaches friendship in a different way. Because he has

INSIGHT

Strangers are friends that you have yet to meet.

—Roberta Lieberman

a different view of Openness, he will always prefer to have just one or two close friends.

> He: *What a week! I'm exhausted.*
>
> She: *Me too. I can't wait for the weekend.*
>
> He: *I've got an idea. . . . Let's get the whole gang together on Saturday and head for the beach.*
>
> She: *(Groan) I thought you said you were tired.*
>
> He: *I am. I've been sitting in my cubicle, chained to my desk all week. This would be a great way to recharge!*
>
> She: *But I spent the whole week doing employee reviews. I've been meeting with people for four straight days. I just want to be alone.*
>
> He: *C'mon, you could stand one more day of people.*
>
> She: *And you could stand one more day alone.*
>
> He: *You know, you could be a little more flexible.*

They're both exhausted—they can agree on that. The weekend is coming, and with it the chance to rest and be refreshed. They both feel the need to restore their Energy, but they will seek to recharge in different ways—and that's when an Openness conflict can begin.

Relaxing at the beach sounds great to *both* of them—but he adds a little something to the suggestion that spoils it for her. *Let's get the whole gang together.* She lets out a groan. To her, relaxing at the beach and getting the whole gang together are mutually exclusive.

The man in this scenario is really not an extrovert—but he has been *sitting in his cubicle, chained to his desk all week.* And his wife is not normally an introvert; she has just been *meeting with people for four straight days.* Sometimes our circumstances and environment influence our approach to Sociability and Energy. Introverts can go stir crazy, and extroverts can get tired of people. A privacy-seeking husband may unexpectedly throw a shindig, and a party-animal wife may suddenly lock her door.

The side you take in an Openness conflict is not always predictable. Sometimes it all comes down to the kind of week you've had.

Have Sociability and Energy been behind some of *your* recurring conflicts? Take our Openness Inventory to find out . . .

"Jack's just recharging. People drain him."

OPENNESS INVENTORY—Sociability	YOU	MATE
Who would like to have people remember his birthday with a party of some kind?		
Who would like to invite the new neighbors over for dessert?		
Who initiates most of the social events in the home?		
Who is more concerned about being included and liked?		
Who worries more about your children not having enough friends?		
Who is more eager to check e-mail and voice mail for messages?		
Who is more embarrassed by standing alone at a party?		
Who stays in better touch with long-distance friends and relatives?		

OPENNESS INVENTORY—Energy	YOU	MATE
Who would prefer to talk through a project with others rather than work on it alone?		
Who feels encouraged and happy at the end of a party, and afterward is ready to talk about what everybody said?		
Who prefers to spend time off with other people?		
Who would rather talk about people than talk about tasks?		
Who still has more to discuss at the end of the day?		
Who likes to get the opinions of other people before making a final decision?		
Who would more likely shrivel up working alone in a cubicle?		

Finding the Root

On a scale from one to ten, how important is Openness to you? Place an X where you think you belong. Now put an O where you think your mate belongs.

1   **10**

Are there recurring arguments in your marriage that you think might be driven by the differences between you and your mate in the area of Openness? What are they about?

Do you think there is something from your past that makes your approach to Openness especially important to you? Have you ever discussed this with your mate?

Do you think there is something from your past that makes Openness especially *difficult* for you? Have you ever discussed this with your mate?

Do you think there is something happening in your life right now that could be reinforcing your approach to Openness?

Dreaming Together: Openness

Everyone loves a Sociable person, but Openness has its liabilities when it's taken to the extreme.

THE **GOOD** SIDE OF OPENNESS	THE **DARK** SIDE OF OPENNESS
Many friends	Superficial friends
Loves people	Hates tasks
Loves company	Avoids solitude
Wants to be included	Manipulates to be included
Treasures friends	Ignores spouse
Motivated by groups	Lacks individual discipline

A Tip for Open Personalities

If you thrive in social situations and feel energized by people, it's hard to understand a mate who constantly seeks time to be alone. You can take a giant first step toward the fence if you will *make sure she has time to recharge.*

Statistically, 75 percent of people are Open personalities; they enjoy Sociability and draw Energy from interaction with others. What a great personality trait—who wouldn't want to be considered Sociable? But try as they might, introverts are exhausted by people and require time to recharge alone—though their desire for seclusion is sometimes a source of guilt. Keirsey and Bates write, "Introverts have reported that they have gone through much of their lives believing that they *ought* to want more sociability. . . . As a result, the introvert seldom provides adequately for his very legitimate desire for territoriality, for breathing room, without experiencing a vague feeling of guilt." [3]

You can relieve your mate's feelings of guilt or shame simply by recognizing that her desire for breathing room is not selfishness or snobbery or social awkwardness. It is a "very legitimate desire for territoriality." It's critical to remember that introverts like people too—but because people drain them of Energy, they need time to recharge before they're ready to face people again.

Remember this situation from earlier in this chapter? A husband and wife were thinking ahead to the upcoming weekend . . .

> *He: What a week! I'm exhausted.*
>
> *She: Me too. I can't wait for the weekend.*
>
> *He: I've got an idea . . . Let's get the whole gang together on Saturday and head for the beach.*
>
> *She: (Groan) I thought you said you were tired.*

He's ready for a party, and she's ready to collapse. This would be a good time for this Sociable husband to apply our principle . . .

> *He: I've got an idea . . . Let's get the whole gang together on Saturday and head for the beach.*
>
> *She: (Groan) I thought you said you were tired.*
>
> *He: I forgot—you've been doing employee reviews all week, haven't you? You need some downtime. How about this: Friday night is all yours. I'll unplug the phone, and you can have the apartment all to yourself. Then we can talk about Saturday, okay?*

If you want to encourage your mate to be more Sociable, then *make sure she has time to recharge.* In the process, you just might recognize your own need for a little "alone time" too.

A Tip for Spouses of Open Personalities

If Sociability is not your natural instinct, and if people have a way of tiring you out, then you can take a step toward your mate's Sociable world by *seeking to expand your boundaries.*

Married couples often experience the phenomenon of *polarization,* the tendency for one person to adjust her personality in response to her mate's. If a Security-oriented woman marries a man who never thinks about Protection and Provision, the woman may tend to become even *more* Security-conscious herself. She feels that she has no choice. Since he doesn't care about Security, she feels that she has to care all the more.

Nowhere is this tendency to polarize more common than with the issue of Openness. *He* continually seeks the company of others, so *she* persistently seeks to withdraw. He can't wait to get out of the house, so she can't wait to get home. They both want to recharge, but neither one feels energized because they've polarized. They've faced off over their respective needs and desires, and now they're involved in an endless tug-of-war that neither one can win.

A tug-of-war is a struggle to pull away from one another—but the struggle ends if one partner decides to step *forward*. That's what this principle is all about: You can put an end to your tug-of-war over Openness by *seeking to expand your boundaries*.

When you look ahead to the weekend, your natural preference might be to spend Friday night curled up alone with a good book. Instead, why not suggest dinner with another couple? Not a party or a huge group gathering, and not an entire evening in the company of others—just dinner. And when you see a free evening coming, why not recommend inviting the neighbors over for dessert? Not *all* the neighbors, just one other couple, and not even for dinner this time—just for dessert.

> **INSIGHT**
> The great thing about marriage is that it enables one to be alone without feeling loneliness.
> —*Gerald Brenan*

These are small steps, and they certainly won't satisfy all the social desires of your people-hungry mate. But they *will* let him know that you are not a recluse, that you like people too, and that you're willing to move toward his world.

Let's return to the couple who were attempting to plan a weekend outing at the beach. If you remember the end of the dialogue, you probably noticed that they didn't get very far. They ended up as they always do, in a tug-of-war over their different desires for Openness.

He: *I've been sitting in my cubicle chained to my desk all week. This would be a great way to recharge!*

She: *But I spent the whole week doing employee reviews. I've been meeting with people for four straight days. I just want to be alone.*

He: *C'mon, you could stand one more day of people.*

She: *And you could stand one more day alone.*

But suppose the woman made a conscious choice to put an end to the tug-of-war by choosing to expand her boundaries ever-so-slightly. She might have said something like this:

He: C'mon, you could stand one more day of people.

She: I'm not sure I could stand a whole group of people. Can I make a suggestion? Let's just invite one other couple to come along. How about Joe and Lysa? We know them well. As tired as I am, I'd rather not invite a lot of strangers. How does that sound?

He wants to get the whole gang together, and she suggests just Joe and Lysa. It may not sound like much, but even this small compromise can help strike a balance between an introvert's and an extrovert's desires. By *seeking to expand your boundaries* to include other people, even a few people at a time, you can begin to relieve the tug-of-war and conserve your Energy at the same time.

Security

Loyalty

Responsibility

Caring

Order

Openness

CONNECTION

THE DIFFERENCES THAT DIVIDE

"Of course those are my socks. After all these years
you'd think you'd learn to recognize my socks."

7 CONNECTION:

STYLES OF COMMUNICATION
and DECISION MAKING

Tim: Joy and I weren't married very long before we realized that we attempt to Connect in different ways. We used to have a lot of conversations that went like this . . .

Joy: "Did you have a nice phone call with your mom this afternoon?"

Tim: "Sure."

Joy: "How is she?"

Tim: "Fine."

Joy: "You weren't on the phone very long. How did she sound?"

Tim: "How did she sound? Uh . . . far away."

Joy: "I mean, did she sound happy or sad or tired—you know, how did she sound?"

Tim: "She sounded fine. By the way, who were you talking to on the phone all this time?"

Joy: "My parents."

Tim: "For an entire hour? What in the world did you talk about? I can't think of that much to say in a week!"

Joy: "I don't know. We just talk about things."

Tim: "I could never talk to my parents for an hour."

Joy: "Why not?"

Tim: "I run out of things to talk about after the first three minutes."

Joy: "You don't have to talk about world issues—just talk to them."

Tim: "But I have to talk to them about something. What would I talk about?"

Joy: "Different things."

Tim: "Like what?"

Joy: "I talked to my parents about all the new flowers and plants they just planted."

Tim: "Flowers and plants? How can you talk for a whole hour about plants?"

Joy: "I don't mind talking about flowers and plants because I'm talking to them. Besides, we talked about other things too. We talked about you and the kids, and my brother, and the neighbors, and the American Legion team, and my dad's paintings, and my mom visiting the shut-ins from church, and the deer that have been coming into the backyard, and their trip to Newfoundland, and their new car, and my old high school's football team, and the weather."

Tim: (Long pause) "I talked to my mom about the weather too."

Joy: "Really? How is the weather there?"

Tim: "Fine."

Communicating to Connect

When different kinds of computers have to communicate, it sometimes leads to problems. They may be running at different speeds, or they may be speaking different languages altogether. Entire corporations exist to help ensure that computers are able to converse. Unfortunately, the same level of technical support is not available to husbands and wives, who often experience precisely the same difficulty with *Connection*.

Here are some comments from couples who have difficulty finding a way to Connect . . .

- *I don't understand his lack of emotion in trials.*

- *I wish she would use less emotion and more facts.*

- *He seems too domineering because he thinks too quickly.*

- *I don't understand why she walks into a store and stops right at the entrance to talk.*

- *It takes me awhile to verbalize my feelings. I need time to process conflict and not feel like I have to rush through it when I'm not ready.*

- *I wish she understood that my words aren't forged in stone. I am just trying to find the words. I'm trying to find out what I feel.*

- *I don't understand why decisions can take so long and be so difficult to make.*

- *He doesn't understand my need to discuss an issue with more than one conversation and on more than one occasion!*

- *He tends to become frustrated easily if a solution is not immediately forthcoming, and he withdraws.*

- *I'm not necessarily out for a specific answer; I just want to dialogue about possible solutions.*

- *I wish he would be more aggressive and open instead of having to talk for two hours to get to his true feelings.*

Connection conflicts can begin about any topic at all, but they quickly shift from the *content* of the discussion to its *style*. The argument is no longer about what you're saying, but how you're saying it—or *not* saying it. A Connection conflict makes it difficult to hear what your mate is saying at all.

Conflicting Communication Styles

Connection problems arise when couples have different styles of *Communication* and *Decision Making*. Your *Communication* style is the *way* you seek to interact. Your style of interaction can be a bigger source of conflict than the actual words you choose. Unfortunately, couples are often completely unaware of the way they instinctively seek to Connect. Our natural style of Communication is one of our most persistent blind spots.

Conflicting Decision-Making Styles

Your *Decision-Making* style is the way you choose between options great and small, from an order at the drive-through to the purchase of a home. There are hundreds of life-changing decisions that husbands and wives must make together and countless minor choices to be resolved each day. Great frustration can result when couples approach decisions along very different paths. As a result, many couples avoid making decisions together at all. They just divide major decisions between them—and then live with the anger and disappointment that result when one partner makes an undesirable choice.

The Root of Other Conflicts

Connection problems are sometimes the most serious hidden issues, because they may underlie the other six. Until we resolve our differences in style, it may be impossible to resolve our differences in substance. In the scenarios that follow, we'll illustrate each of the conflicting Communication and Decision-Making styles and give you a sense of the frustration and confusion they can produce—that is, if you don't know already.

Conflicting Communication Styles

Three pairs of conflicting Communication styles are common between married couples: *linear vs. circular, emotional vs. cognitive,* and *interactive vs. didactic.*

Linear vs. Circular Communicators

He: *Did you see Nate's teacher today?*

She: *I stopped by the school about noon. I thought I'd never get there—the lunchtime traffic was unbelievable! There's a building site near there and . . .*

He: *What did the teacher say?*

She: *She said he'll have to stay after school tomorrow. Have you been in that school lately? It's practically falling apart. Some of the ceiling tiles are—*

He: *Why does he have to stay after?*

She: *I don't like the idea of him sitting alone in that dark old classroom. Why should he be the only one who—*

He: *WHY DOES HE HAVE TO STAY AFTER?*

He orders his thoughts carefully before he speaks and then presents his ideas in a clear, concise, and orderly fashion—and he expects his wife to do the same in return. But often she doesn't. To him, she seems to speak as she thinks, and she stops to explore detours and rabbit trails as she pleases on the road to her eventual conclusion. This is the tension between *linear vs. circular* styles of Communication.

To the linear communicator, the destination is the thing, and he wants to find the shortest path to the goal. To the circular communicator, the trip itself is what it's all about, and you might as well relax and enjoy the ride.

INSIGHT

It's all right to hold a conversation, but you should let go of it now and then.

—Richard Armour

He wants a report on the meeting with Nate's teacher. *I stopped by the school about noon,* she begins— then suddenly her focus shifts to lunchtime traffic and roadside construction. He brings her back to the subject, and she resumes her report once again—then her attention inexplicably jumps to the condition of the school building. His frustration is steadily growing. Will she *ever* land this plane?

Though he doesn't recognize it, each of her detours *does* have something to do with the topic. Lunchtime traffic and roadside construction *did* play a role in her visit with the teacher, and the crumbling school building is a part of her concern for her son. But that isn't what he wants to hear. He came to this conversation with a three-point outline in mind: *Did you see Nate's teacher? What did the teacher say? Why does he have to stay after?*

Linear communicators cannot bear the seemingly pointless meanderings of their circular partners. They find them illogical, wasteful, and draining, and that's why linear communicators are always interrupting to edit, summarize, or speed the story along. They want the facts, ma'am, *just* the facts. But to circular communicators, their linear spouses seem impatient, uncaring, and rude. They don't care about what you want to say; they only care about what they want to hear. Circular communicators fear that once they give their linear partners the facts, they will totally tune them out since they now have all the information they wanted. Linear and circular communicators approach a discussion with different goals in mind: She wants *conversation,* but he only wants *information.*

They're both concerned about Nate, but they're having trouble communicating about it. They have a bad *Connection.*

Emotional vs. Cognitive Communicators

> She: *Did you see the news? There was a major airline disaster today.*
>
> He: *Huh.*
>
> She: *Did you hear what I said?*
>
> He: *You said there was an airline disaster.*
>
> She: *That's right. Two hundred people were on board and there were no survivors. Men, women, children—whole families perished. The photos were awful!*
>
> He: *Huh.*
>
> She: *Is that all you can say? "Huh"?*
>
> He: *Uh . . . that's bad.*

A major airline disaster. Think of the lives shattered, the careers ended, the families split apart; think of the men, women, and children lost; think of the fear, the panic, the final moments of agony. She shares this gut-wrenching horror with her husband, whose heart pours out in response . . . *Huh.*

This is the contrast between *emotional vs. cognitive* communicators. She responds to news of the catastrophe with passion, her thoughts and emotions combining to give a heartfelt and compassionate response. The news of the airline disaster is more than a fact to be comprehended; it's a tragedy to be *experienced.*

But he responds to the tragedy as he responds to *all* problems—he holds it at arm's length and studies it. He approaches the subject logically, factually, creeping cautiously up to the edge and peering over, always careful not to get sucked into the quicksand of surrounding emotion.

INSIGHT

The opposite of talking isn't listening. The opposite of talking is waiting.

—*Fran Lebowitz*

141

To her, emotion is part of her thinking. To him, emotion *interferes* with his thinking. She thinks and feels at virtually the same instant; he thinks first and feels later—sometimes *much* later. His cognitive style drives her crazy; she feels as if she's talking to a stenographer instead of another human being. *Is that all you can say?* From the depths of his soul comes, *Uh . . . that's bad.*

Emotional communicators find their cognitive partners cold, distant, and disconnected. Cognitive communicators think their compassionate mates are just overreacting. If she would just stop to *think* first, she might be able to keep things in *perspective* . . .

He kept the airline disaster at arm's length, but he may not find it as easy to do with the Connection conflict that's coming his way.

Interactive vs. Didactic Communicators

He: *Your folks called today. They bought one of those—*

She: *Bread makers?*

He: *That's right. They said that they—*

She: *Do they like it?*

He: *Yes, they said they like it. It has one of those—*

She: *Dough hooks?*

He: *No, one of those—*

She: *Delay timers? Those are really handy.*

He: *Would you let me finish a sentence?*

Some think of conversation like a formal dinner, where dishes are served to you one at a time and your only job is to keep your seat and wait. Others think of conversation as a buffet where you take what you want when you want it. These are the contrasting styles of *interactive vs. didactic* Communication.

Didactic communicators think of dialogue as a series of presentations: First *you* talk, then *I* talk. Conversations should operate according to democratic principles of justice and fair play. You speak your piece, you wait your turn, and it's never polite to interrupt. But interactive communicators recognize no such rules. To them, a conversation is a *group* activity. If you have a question, throw it in. If you have a comment, voice it—even if the other person happens to be *talking* at the time.

He begins a presentation. *Your folks called today. They bought one of those* . . . But he hesitates for a split second, and to his interactive wife, that sounds like an invitation to jump right in. *Bread makers?* She finishes the sentence for him. To an interactive communicator, that's just being helpful.

He begins again, and this time she interjects a question. Next, she guesses at the ending of another partial sentence. She guesses wrong, so she tries again. She's having a wonderful time interacting, but he's finding it impossible to complete his presentation. *Would you let me finish a sentence?*

> **INSIGHT**
> To do all the talking and not be willing to listen is a form of greed.
> —*Democritus of Abdera*

The husband thinks his wife is being rude and impatient. But she isn't trying to be rude; she sees her interactive style as a sign of genuine interest and enthusiasm. Conversations are never dull when she's around. By contrast, her didactic husband can seem formal, stuffy, and downright boring. He seems to be more interested in what *he* has to say than in what anyone has to say in reply. That doesn't sound like a conversation to her—it sounds more like a speech.

He wants to speak, and she wants to interact.

Decision-Making Styles

There are three pairs of conflicting Decision-Making styles that are common to couples: *decisive vs. tentative, intuitive vs. evidential,* and *final vs. open-ended.*

Decisive vs. Tentative Decision Makers

Here's another couple who's having trouble establishing a Connection.

She: *So are we going to Disney World or Universal Studios?*
He: *I like Disney World. But I also like Universal . . .*
She: *We said Disney World was better for the kids.*
He: *That's right, it is . . . I suppose.*
She: *Then let's go for it!*
He: *I just want to look at the brochures once more.*

She: You know, you are driving me nuts.

He: Maybe we should look at Epcot too . . .

It's vacation time, and they have to decide together on a getaway location. What will it be—Disney World or Universal Studios? There's a lot riding on this decision: the kids' enjoyment, their own satisfaction, the best use of their limited funds. And when are they ever going to have a chance like this again? So many choices—and so many possible regrets.

Somehow, it's an easy decision for her. It's not that there's only one clear option—either choice would be fine for her. She just wants to *decide.* But her husband will agonize over this decision. Again and again he will consider all options while avoiding a final commitment. This is the difference between the *decisive vs. tentative* styles of Decision Making.

I like Disney World. But I also like Universal Studios, he waffles. This is not the first time they've had this discussion. *We said Disney World was better for the kids,* she reminds him. He offers the slightest hint of a possible decision: *That's right, it is . . . I suppose . . .* and she's on it like an attack dog. *Then let's go for it!*

Tentative Decision Makers tend to focus on the *outcome* of their choices. Is this the best thing we can do? Are there better options we've overlooked? Have we missed anything in our Decision-Making process? What will it cost us if our decision turns out to be the wrong one? With so much at stake, it's no wonder some Decision Makers have a hard time making a final choice.

But *decisive* Decision Makers tend to concentrate on the decision itself. For them, an unfinalized decision is like a half-finished project or an unmade bed. There's a sense of completion that comes with a final decision, and they want to get it done. Enough of this endless discussion; let's just *decide,* even if it means sacrificing money or quality.

This tentative husband and decisive wife are like two people on either side of a door—one is trying to hold it open while the other is trying to pull it shut. With that approach, they may be vacationing at home this year.

Intuitive vs. Evidential Decision Makers

> She: So what do you think? The Ford or the Honda?
>
> He: The Ford. Definitely.
>
> She: Why?
>
> He: I just have a feeling about this. Trust me.
>
> She: I looked at Consumer Reports . . . *they say the Honda has a better repair record. But then I checked the Blue Book online, and the Ford holds its value better . . .*
>
> He: The Ford. No doubt about it.
>
> She: How can you be so sure?
>
> He: My gut tells me. I'm never wrong about these things.
>
> She: I'd feel a lot better if your gut would look at some evidence.

He thinks they should buy the Ford. He's not *half*-certain, or *almost* sure—he knows. *The Ford. No doubt about it.* But if you pressed him on the *source* of his confidence, he'd have a hard time telling you. This is not the first car he's purchased, and he has some knowledge of automobiles, but his certainty comes more from an inner feeling, an intuitive sense that tells him this is the right choice. *My gut tells me.*

But to his wife, the way to approach a major decision is by reading, researching, and gathering data. Never mind what your gut tells you; what do the *facts* say? She might consider listening to her gut too, but only after *her* gut has taken the time to consider some objective evidence. *I'm never wrong about these things,* her husband says. His wife remembers differently. Sometimes he *is* wrong about these things, but that's not enough to suppress his inner sense of confidence and conviction. These are the contrasting styles of *intuitive vs. evidential* Decision Makers.

Evidential Decision Makers approach decisions by looking *outward*. They know that an objective evaluation of all the available evidence will give them the greatest possible chance of making a good decision. But intuitive Decision Makers see this as unnecessary. They know that facts can be manipulated and research can be endless and exhausting. Ultimately, you still have to *decide*. What does your gut tell you?

Intuitive Decision Makers find an evidential approach to be tedious,

> ### The Word
> He who guards his mouth and his tongue, guards his soul from troubles.
>
> PROVERBS 21:23

boring, and redundant. But evidential Decision Makers, who lack that inner sense of confidence, find an intuitive approach to be subjective, superficial, and unreliable. When one partner won't trust her instincts and the other won't listen to reason, it can be hard to make a decision about anything.

Final vs. Open-ended Decision Makers

She: I bought this blouse today. How do you like it?

He: I love it. It's perfect for you.

She: Do you really like it? It was on sale, 40 percent off.

He: Sounds like a good deal. You can't beat 40 percent off.

She: I wonder . . . I bought it at a department store, and sometimes they have bigger sales over at the outlet mall.

He: Look, you already bought the blouse, so forget about it. It's a done deal.

She: I'm just going to run over to the outlet mall and take a look.

She made a purchase today, but not a *final* purchase. For her, decisions are seldom final—they're always open to reconsideration. Some people make an ultimate decision and then never look back. But others are less certain about the choices they've made, and they like to revisit them from time to time to either regret or rejoice. These are the different styles of the *final vs. open-ended* Decision Makers.

She has every reason to think she made a good decision about her blouse. *It was on sale, 40 percent off.* Her husband agrees, and he looks for every opportunity to help solidify her decision. *I love it. It's perfect for you. You can't beat 40 percent off.* The decision is over, but to her it's not *final.* It's an open-ended event that needs to be revisited to make doubly sure that it was the best thing to do—even if that means continuing to shop for the blouse after the purchase has been made.

Think again about the three pairs of Decision-Making styles we've considered. The *decisive vs. tentative* styles affect the way we first approach a decision; the *intuitive vs. evidential* styles influence the way we make the decision itself; but the *final vs. open-ended* styles don't come into play until after a decision has already been made.

She once bought new curtains for the house; it took her a week to make the selection, and she revisited her decision for another month. He once bought a bass boat; it took him fifteen minutes and he never thought about it again. It's not that he makes better decisions than his wife; it's just that he has a different attitude toward the decisions he makes. For her, a decision is always open-ended. For him, all sales are final.

Even couples who agree on their decisions may not agree about their feelings after the choice has been made. Before, during, and after a decision, it's better if you can make a Connection.

Once again it's time to consider how this issue relates to you. What is your natural style of Communication and Decision Making? Take the following Connection Inventory to help decide . . .

DOWNS

"I can too be spontaneous! I just like a little advance notice."

CONNECTION INVENTORY—Communication Style	YOU	MATE
Who is more eager to get to the point without a lot of detail?		
Who finds it more difficult or tedious to make conversation if it isn't about an issue or task that interests her?		
Who has more trouble thinking of questions to ask and then genuinely listening to the answers?		
Who is quicker to try to fix a situation after hearing the problem?		
Who would rather deal with facts than emotions?		
Who gets more frustrated if the details of a story are not clear and accurate?		

CONNECTION INVENTORY— Decision-Making Style	YOU	MATE
Who makes decisions faster?		
Who feels the need to look at more options before making a decision?		
Who seems more confident after the decision has been made and feels fewer regrets?		
Who feels less of a need to look at research and other information before making a decision?		
Who sometimes makes a decision without even consulting his mate?		
Who is less likely to agonize over major decisions?		
Who would rather make a decision for the sake of convenience, preferring to save time rather than find the highest quality or the best deal?		

Finding the Root

What is your natural Communication style? Place an X on each continuum where you think you belong. Then place an O where you think your mate belongs.

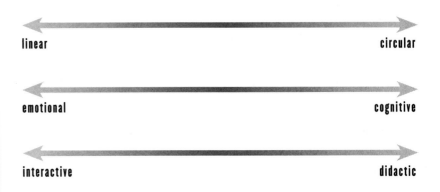

What is your natural Decision-Making style? Place an X on each continuum where you think you belong. Then place an O where you think your mate belongs.

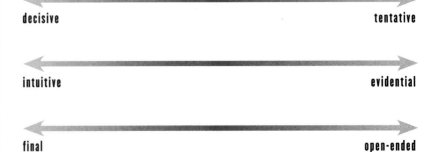

Are there recurring arguments in your marriage that you think are the direct result of poor Connection? What are they about?

Do you think there is something from your past that makes your desire for quality Connection especially important to you? Have you ever discussed this with your mate?

Do you think there is something from your past that makes Connection especially *difficult* for you? Have you ever discussed this with your mate?

Do you think there is something happening in your life right now that could be heightening your desire for better Connection?

Dreaming Together: Connection

As we said before, Connection conflicts are sometimes the hardest because they underlie all of the other arguments. It's hard to resolve a disagreement when you can't even make a good Connection. Every style of Communication and Decision Making has a dark side associated with it.

The Word

There is more hope for a fool than for someone who speaks without thinking.

PROVERBS 29:20 NLT

THE STYLE OF CONNECTION	THE **DARK** SIDE OF THIS STYLE OF CONNECTION
Linear communicator	Boring
Circular communicator	Distracted
Cognitive communicator	Passionless
Emotional communicator	Impulsive
Didactic communicator	Rigid
Interactive communicator	Rude
Decisive decision maker	Impetuous
Tentative decision maker	Vacillating
Intuitive decision maker	Biased
Evidential decision maker	Rationalistic
Final decision maker	Inflexible
Open-ended decision maker	Noncommittal

Tips for Different Kinds of Communicators

Once you've identified your own natural style of Communication, it's important to begin to communicate in a way that your spouse can appreciate—important, that is, if you really want to make a Connection.

A *linear communicator* can *remind himself what conversation is for.* For him, the purpose of conversation is information, but for her the purpose is *interaction.* Instead of pushing ahead for the facts, he can stop and ask himself, "Do we understand each other? Are we making a good Connection?"

A *circular communicator* can *learn to begin with a summary statement*: "Yes, I saw Nate's teacher today, and Nate has to stay after school tomorrow because he failed his math test." With the facts in hand, the linear partner can now sit back and more easily enjoy the ride.

No one would think it unreasonable if his mate asked him to speak louder or more clearly. Volume and clarity are two qualities that help make a message intelligible. Emotion can help too; a *cognitive communicator's* message would come through a lot clearer if he would *tell his emotional partner not only what he thinks but how he feels*. He can begin to practice the discipline of asking himself, "How do I *feel* about this?"

Emotional communicators can help their cognitive partners by *helping them recognize their emotions*. After they give you the facts, ask some questions. If "How do you feel?" seems a little too frontal, instead try "How does that strike you?" or even "What do you think about that?" By asking him what he thinks *about* his thoughts, his emotions might begin to enter the picture too.

Didactic communicators can resist the temptation to deliver a lecture by *interrupting themselves*. Instead of waiting to be interrupted and then becoming impatient or frustrated, they can break up their own monologue with questions or requests for feedback. "What do you think?" "Do you know what I mean?"

> **INSIGHT**
> Much—even most—meaning in conversation does not reside in the words spoken at all, but is filled by the person listening.
> —*Julia Wood*

Interactive communicators can *let their partners know they have a question or comment without actually interrupting the conversation*—at least, not for long. "Remind me to ask you something" is another way of saying, "I'd like to interject something here, but I know you don't like to be interrupted, so I'll save it until you're finished."

Tips for Different Kinds of Decision Makers

Decisive and *tentative* decision makers can *agree together in advance on a deadline for a decision*. The deadline allows the decisive partner to know that there will be an eventual end to her tentative partner's procrastination, and it gives the tentative partner the freedom to think things over without feeling pressured or hurried prior to the deadline. It also helps the decisive partner to *lighten up*; there's no sense trying to hurry things along when the decision isn't due for another week.

Intuitive and *evidential* decision makers can *discuss in advance how their decision will be made*. By focusing on the decision itself, rather than on what the decision will be, they can make sure they allow room for both evidence and intuition. They can decide what research will be helpful, who will gather it, and what the limits of their fact-gathering will be. They can agree as to when the research phase will be over and when the decision making can begin.

Final and *open-ended* decision makers have no problem agreeing to *make* a decision; their problem is agreeing about the decision once it's *done.* Final decision makers can *agree to a review period,* sort of like a thirty-day money-back guarantee on a purchase. The open-ended partner has thirty days to agonize, reflect, and reconsider a decision— after that, it's done. In this way, second-guessing becomes an intentional part of the decision-making process itself.

"Which one of you would you say is the risk taker in the relationship?"

WHAT ARE WE FIGHTING FOR?

In doing the original research for this book, we interviewed hundreds of couples about the topics they most often disagreed about in their marriage. We found ourselves having a recurring conversation that went something like this:

Us: *Tell us about the things in your marriage that you seem to argue about over and over again.*

She: *We don't argue in our marriage.*

He: *No, we don't. Not really.*

Us: *Oh. Okay . . . So you agree about everything?*

She: *Oh no, we disagree about things.*

He: *We just don't argue. (He takes her hand and they smile at each other)*

She: *Like when he gets ready for church, he gets in the car and pulls out in the driveway and waits for me to come out. (She laughs)*

He: *I guess we do disagree about that. (He laughs too) I just think it's important to respect other people's time. When she makes me wait, it's like she's saying, "Your time is unimportant, so you can wait for me."*

She: *(Dropping his hand) Well, if you'd help get the kids ready instead of sitting in the car testing out the horn, we might be ready sooner.*

He: *So it's the kids' fault? Then why does this happen even when the kids aren't around? What's your excuse then?*

Us: *(Taking notes furiously) Please tell us more about the way you don't argue.*

We Never Argue

Our research has taught us that just as prisons are filled with innocent people, Christian marriages are filled with couples who never argue. Oh, they *disagree* from time to time; they may differ or squabble or bicker or even have a tiff—but they definitely do not argue. We found Christian couples to be a walking thesaurus when it comes to "arguing." They seem to do everything else *but.*

As we said at the beginning of the book, the very presence of conflict in marriage is a source of embarrassment and even shame for Christians.

Don't misunderstand us—we've all had disagreements in our marriages that we *should* be ashamed of, because of their style or intensity or because of the foolish and hurtful things we did or said. But we have found that Christians are often ashamed that conflict is there at all, regardless of how it's handled. Christians tend to see conflict as fundamentally incompatible with romantic love, commitment, and spiritual maturity. Arguing seems to have no place in a truly Christian marriage. The ideal marriage is thought to have no conflict at all.

This commonly held conviction only deepens with the passage of time. It seems only natural that we should disagree from time to time when we're first married, but surely we should have worked this out by *now*. The only possible explanation for our ongoing disagreement is sin, or stubbornness, or maybe even a fundamental weakness in the marriage itself. Maybe we were never right for each other at all.

In marriage, as in life, attitude is crucial. One of the chief goals of this book is to encourage you to adopt a new attitude toward your differences. In the same way, the purpose of this final chapter is to encourage you to consider an entirely new attitude toward conflict and the role it plays in marriage. Yes, we all argue at times in inappropriate ways, and yes, we could all stand to reduce the amount of conflict in our marriages—but we want you to consider a different attitude toward conflict *itself*. We cannot emphasize enough the importance of this attitudinal shift. This is far more than trying to apply the "power of positive thinking" or trying to see a half-empty glass as half-full. *This is an attempt to re-understand what marriage is supposed to be and the necessary role that conflict plays in it.*

Why is this attitude adjustment so important? Because if we view conflict only as a negative activity, as never more than the manifestation of sinfulness or selfishness or pride, then our response to conflict when it occurs will always be negative. We'll seek to deny it, ignore it, or run from it—anything to make it just go away. In fact, this is precisely what most of us do. Researchers tell us that the most common ways couples deal with marital conflict are through conquest, avoidance, bargaining, or a quick fix.

But how are we supposed to take on a new attitude toward conflict?

INSIGHT

When couples who report that they "never argue" are interviewed separately, one partner frequently admits that he or she has developed a pattern of "peace at any price" and the price is usually the loss of self.

—*Rebecca Cutter,* When Opposites Attract

FOUR
**Common Stages
of Conflict in
Marriage**

1
JUST MARRIED:
Have it your way

2
YEARS 1–2:
Have it my way

3
YEARS 2–10:
Have it our way

4
AFTER 10 YEARS:
Have it any way you want

How do we begin to think in a positive way about something that's been such a source of anger, frustration, and regret? We might as well have called this chapter "The Stomach Flu: Give It Another Chance," or "Satan: Not Such a Bad Guy After All." How in the world do we learn to accept the unacceptable?

Rethinking Conflict in Marriage

The place to begin is not by looking at conflict but by stepping back and taking a fresh look at marriage itself. We'd like you to consider five revolutionary ideas—thoroughly biblical ideas—that can change the way you look at conflict in your marriage.

Revolutionary Idea #1: God Is Not Finished with You Yet

Several years ago, there was a poster that was very popular. It said:

> *I am not on this earth to change you,*
> *And you are not on this earth to change me.*
> *But if our paths should cross*
> *And our lives should touch,*
> *It is beautiful.*

On first reading it sounds noble and even a bit profound, but it's hard to imagine a more unbiblical sentiment—especially for married couples. For those of us who have entered the covenant of marriage, there should be a poster more like this:

> *I am on this earth to change you,*
> *And you are on this earth to change me—*
> *Not by criticizing or demanding,*
> *But by seeking to truly know and love each other.*
> *If we spend the next thirty, forty, or fifty years together*
> *And are not better human beings because of it,*
> *May God forgive us both.*

How does our little poster strike you? It isn't likely to become a bestseller, because it flies in the face of a popular understanding of *tolerance*. According to many, no human being is qualified to change the life of another. But according to the Bible, *no human being is qualified to remain as he is.*

The Bible tells us that though God loves us, He is not yet *finished* with us—any more than we are finished with our own children. We love our kids, and we accept them for who they are, but we still want them to mature and grow in a hundred different ways. We're not always sure what the finished product should look like, but we're sure of what we *don't* see. It isn't hard to recognize that our children, regardless of their ages, still have a lot of growing up to do. God wants the same for us. Maybe that's why it's been said, "Marriage is the last chance God gives you to grow up."

God wants us to grow, too, regardless of our ages—and He has a very clear picture of what the finished product should look like. We are to grow to look more and more like His own Son—like God Himself in human form—and marriage plays a tremendous role in this growth process.

Dan Allender and Tremper Longman, in their excellent book *Intimate Allies,* write:

> **INSIGHT**
> Often we change jobs, friends, and spouses instead of ourselves.
> —*Akbaraki H. Jetha*

> Marriages can become plodding, cyclical routines filled with boredom and obligation. No one expects that a marriage will retain the giddy glow of excitement that comes with the novelty of new love. But it is equally wrong to assume that passion must wane simply because of familiarity. True passion comes from the nature of the purpose of a marriage.[1]

Marriage can become a boring routine—but it doesn't have to. Contrary to popular opinion, it's possible for a couple to share passion even after years of married life together. By "passion" we mean much more than simple sexual desire. Passion is the consuming fire of life. Think of it as enthusiasm or eagerness or *gusto*—an ancient Italian word that means "a taste for life." *Passion* is perhaps the one word we would most like to describe our lives—and our marriages too. But where does passion come from? In marriage, passion comes from a clear understanding of what marriage is *for*.

"The purpose of every marriage," Allender and Longman write, "is to shape the raw material of life to reveal more fully the glory of God."[2] And just what are the "raw materials" that marriage is intended to shape? First and foremost, those raw materials are *you*.

The idea that we should be willing to be changed by our partner is viewed by many as intolerant—but the view that we should be *unwilling* to be changed by one another is viewed by the Bible as supremely *arrogant*. God loves us, and He will never leave us—but He will never leave us *alone*, either. He is not finished with us yet.

Revolutionary Idea #2: Marriage Is One of the Tools God Uses to Shape Us

One of the questions we like to ask at marriage conferences is, "What do you think marriage is *for*?" We get a lot of blank stares when we ask that one, as if we were asking, "What are legs for?" or "Why should you breathe?" It's a question that doesn't seem to *need* an answer. Marriage isn't really *for* anything, is it? We marry for the same reason we climb a mountain—because it's *there*.

Actually, "What is marriage for?" is a critical question. Your answer to that question would tell us a lot about your level of satisfaction with your marriage. It's a question of expectations. When we ask, "What is marriage for?" what we're really asking is, "What did you *expect* marriage to be?" Some of us expected marriage to be like an endless date, or like a forty-year love affair, or like a long bike ride coasting downhill with the wind in our hair . . .

Some of us were seriously disappointed.

"What is marriage for?" is a question most couples never ask, yet they have an answer for it nonetheless—an implicit answer. Most couples assume that marriage, like life itself, is to *enjoy*. And if the purpose of marriage is simply to maximize our pleasure, then if we aren't enjoying ourselves, something must be wrong. If marriage is to enjoy, then when we come to a difficult decision, the only relevant question is, "What would please me most?"

And if marriage is only to enjoy, whatever *isn't* pleasurable is an enemy of the marriage—something to be endured, or tolerated, or better yet, avoided altogether. And conflict, it goes without saying, is rarely a barrel of fun.

The Bible's most revolutionary teaching on the subject of marriage is not about roles or commitment or communication; the Bible's most profound insight is that *there is a purpose for marriage.* The purpose of marriage is to glorify God by helping to reshape each of us into the person he or she is intended to be.

As philosopher and psychologist Thomas Moore once said, "Marriage may look like an arrangement of persons, but at a deeper level it is a profound stirring of souls."[3] There is far more to marriage than meets the eye. It may look like a simple living arrangement or social contract, but as Moore says, at a deeper level "it is the creation of a vessel in which soul-making can be accomplished."[4]

Marriage, in other words, is a kind of workshop. It's a woodshop where warped and curling timbers are flattened and splintered surfaces are sanded smooth. It's an auto shop where twisted frames are straightened and crumpled dents are pulled out and filled. It's a blacksmith shop where hammers clang and sparks fly and the hardest of metals are slowly willed into useful shapes. Marriage is the place where we are hammered, molded, and loved into the image of Christ.

In case it's been a few years since you were in a classroom, allow us to remind you: *Learning isn't always fun.* Learning *is* a lot of fun when you're first getting started, because in the beginning it's all Big Bird and Crayolas. But the older you get, the harder the lessons become, and then learning requires more discipline and repetition and some nights a lot of caffeine. The lessons of marriage are no different.

Revolutionary Idea #3: Marriage Will Not Always Be Enjoyable

Workshops are dangerous places with the potential for serious injury. Marriage is no different. Any tool sharp enough to smooth and shape can also rip and wound. Marriage is the ultimate intimacy workshop, and the potential for hurt is very real.

Marriage brings together two people who are created in the image of God. They individually and as a couple reflect divine glory. Marriage is an awesome and wonderful union that has great potential for joy and celebration.

The Bible, though, is a realistic book. It also describes us as flawed,

INSIGHT

A marriage is like a seesaw. Even when one partner acts alone, it affects the other. When you make a change in your behavior or your attitude entirely on your own, you can work a miracle in your marriage.

—*Susan Page in* How One of You Can Bring the Two of You Together selfish creatures; we are sinners. When two sinners come together, they do not become less selfish or less flawed; they become more so. Marriage is a frightening prospect that can be the arena for harm and pain.[5]

INSIGHT

In a successful marriage, there is no such thing as one's way. There is only the way of both, only the bumpy, dusty, difficult, but always mutual path.

—*Phyllis McGinley*

But if marriage is a workshop that can sometimes be an "arena for harm and pain," how are we to protect ourselves? You can avoid the workshop altogether and greatly reduce your risk of injury, just as you can avoid the kitchen and reduce your risk of eating. To refuse to enter the workshop of marriage, which many married couples do, is to refuse to be educated—to refuse to *grow*. Skip the workshop, and you miss what marriage is *for*. No pain—but no gain.

If "Woodshop 101" is not an elective but a required course, then how *do* we protect ourselves from injury? Simply put, *by learning to use the tools properly*. As in all workshops, the greatest risk of danger is not from using the tools but from *misusing* them. The workshop is not a place to be careless. There are tools that every marital workshop should possess and every married person should master.

Revolutionary Idea #4: We Will Sometimes Resent the Role Our Mate Plays

An unpolished gemstone looks no different than an ordinary piece of gravel. To polish it, you need three things: a rock tumbler, some abrasive grit, and at least one other stone. A rock tumbler is little more than a jar lying on its side atop a pair of rollers. A motor powers the rollers; when you turn the tumbler on, the jar begins to roll, and whatever is inside the jar begins to—you guessed it—*tumble*.

Inside the jar you place the stones and some abrasive grit. When the tumbler begins to roll, the rocks will slowly rise up the wall of the jar and then drop, crashing into one another, over and over again. Each time they collide, the grit removes a tiny bit of surface material at the point of impact. Each time they collide, the stones become a little smoother—very, very slowly.

What happens if you forget the abrasive grit? The stones will still collide, but without an abrasive there's nothing to *smooth* the stones. They'll continue to crash into each other—perhaps even chip or damage each other—but the finished product will look no smoother than it did when you began. Thousands of impacts, but no polish.

And what happens if you forget the other stone? Not much. The lone rock will still tumble, but with nothing to strike *against,* it simply rises and falls. There will still be some abrasion as the stone bounces against the side of the jar, but without another stone—without something of equal hardness to strike against—the polishing process could take years instead of weeks.

It isn't always enjoyable to be the other rock in someone else's tumbler. It isn't pleasant to collide with your mate—whether it's over Security or Loyalty or Caring or Connection—and it's even less pleasant when your mate crashes into *you.* But that's the growth process of marriage; God drops two stones of equal hardness into the tumbler of marriage, and *He Himself is the abrasive.* With His help we smooth and polish one another; without Him, we only collide.

This is the strange paradox of marriage. We assume that growth is occurring when everything is going well in marriage, and that conflict always represents a step backward. In fact, it's often just the opposite; we not only grow *despite* our conflicts, we grow *because* of them. "Marriage is an institution of joy and grief," Allender and Longman write. "And the glory often comes through the struggles in communication, goals, priorities, child rearing, and sex. Anyone who expects glory without a fight is foolish."[6]

No one likes to cause friction, but it's a necessary part of the smoothing process. We need to accept the role that our mate is sometimes called to play in our lives, and we need to embrace the process itself. "Faithful are the wounds of a friend," Proverbs 27:6 tells us, and sometimes a wound is the most faithful thing your mate can give.

Revolutionary Idea #5: The Presence of Conflict in Your Marriage Means Nothing

If marriage is for the purpose of molding us into the image of Christ, and if conflict is a necessary part of that process, then it follows that conflict itself is nothing to be ashamed of. But we do *not* mean to suggest that all conflict is a good and acceptable part of marriage! The worst thing we could do is to simply put a gloss over selfish, cruel, and even violent behavior. Our goal in this chapter is to challenge you to change your thinking about conflict *itself,* not to encourage you to glibly accept any and all forms of behavior from your mate—or from yourself.

As we said before, any tool sharp enough to smooth and shape can also rip and wound. We believe that conflict—*badly handled* conflict—can be an extremely destructive force, and we wrote the companion volume to this book, *Fight Fair!,* to teach couples how to conduct a conflict in a peaceful and productive way. The presence of conflict in your marriage means nothing, but the way you conduct yourself in conflict means everything—because the way you and your mate deal with conflict will determine whether you will grow from it or be wounded by it.

The messages we tell ourselves have the power to affect everything we are and do. If we tell ourselves that the only purpose of marriage is personal fulfillment, then we will view all unfulfilling elements of marriage as hindrances to that goal. When conflict arises—unfulfilling as it tends to be—we will deal with it just as we would a flat tire, a broken window, or a nagging headache: We will do as little as is absolutely necessary to make it go away and then return as quickly as possible to the real business of pleasure.

But what if we begin to tell ourselves a *different message*? What if we begin to believe that marriage is actually *for* something, that its purpose is to help reshape us into the people God intends us to be, and that our differing dreams and conflicting personalities can play a positive role in that process? As our thinking changes, so will we. We will begin to respond to conflict just as we would physical exercise or study or practicing a musical instrument. We will become students of conflict rather than avoiders; we will begin to wade into the confusion instead of simply giving up; and we will be willing to endure the occasional collisions for the sake of the polishing that we know is taking place.

A Final Word

Marriage is not a Frequent Flier program. No one is going to award you a free trip to the Bahamas just for logging marital miles. What we long for most, deep in our hearts, is not mere longevity but *love.*

The greatest mistake that a couple can make is to confuse *proximity* with *intimacy. They are not the same.* We yearn for intimacy, and so we marry. Once we're married, we assume that we have automatically achieved our goal. After all, we *live* together, we *sleep* together—how could two people be so close and not be intimate? Sadly, millions of couples can answer that question from firsthand experience.

Marriage makes intimacy possible, but not inevitable. Entering a marriage will not satisfy your hunger for companionship any more than entering a restaurant will satisfy your hunger for food. Too many couples make the mistake of viewing their wedding day as the end of a race—the race to find a mate—instead of hearing the words "I now pronounce you husband and wife" as the starting gun in a lifelong race to achieve intimacy. Every couple begins this race, but not every couple completes it. After fifty years of marriage, every couple crosses a major milestone in that race; sadly, for many, it is not the golden event they had envisioned.

Our goal in writing *One of Us Must Be Crazy* is to encourage couples to take a different attitude toward their fundamental differences—to understand the role that Security, Loyalty, Responsibility, Caring, Order, Openness, and Connection play in our individual lives and in our marriages. Our goal is to help you identify your own dreams, to understand your mate's true motives, to put your differences in perspective, to anticipate areas of disagreement, and to learn to work together as partners in life and love. The ideas and suggestions in this book are only the beginning of a lifelong journey—a journey *away* from the excesses of your own personality and *toward* the strange and mysterious world of your partner in marriage. But the journey of a thousand miles begins with a single step, so remember: The most important thing is that you take a step at all.

NOTES

DIFFERENT PEOPLE, DIFFERENT DREAMS

1. Scott Stanley et al., *A Lasting Promise: A Christian Guide to Fighting for Your Marriage* (San Francisco: Jossey-Bass, 1998), 119, 129, 135.

2. John Gottman and Nan Silver, *The Seven Principles for Making Marriage Work* (New York: Three Rivers Press, 1999), 129.

3. Ibid., 130.

4. Stanley, 119.

5. Clifford Notarius and Howard Markman, *We Can Work It Out: How to Solve Conflicts, Save Your Marriage, and Strengthen Your Love for Each Other* (New York: Putnam, 1993), 153.

LOYALTY

1. Terry Hargrave and Nedra Fetterman, "The Ineffable Us-ness of Marriage," *Psychotherapy Networker* 25, no.4 (July/August 2001): 55–61.

2. Michael Leach and Therese Borchard, eds., *I Like Being Married: Treasured Traditions, Rituals, and Stories* (New York: Doubleday, 2002).

CARING

1. Susan Page, *How One of You Can Bring the Two of You Together: Breakthrough Strategies to Resolve Your Conflicts and Reignite Your Love* (New York: Broadway Books, 1997), 155.

OPENNESS

1. For more on introversion and extroversion, see David Keirsey and Marilyn Bates, *Please Understand Me: Character and Temperament Types* (Del Mar, Calif.: Prometheus Nemesis, 1984), 14–16.

2. Julia Wood, *Interpersonal Communication: Everyday Encounters*, 2d ed. (Belmont, Calif.: Wadsworth, 1999), 253.

3. Keirsey and Bates, 16.

WHAT ARE WE FIGHTING FOR?

1. Dan Allender and Tremper Longman, *Intimate Allies: Rediscovering God's Design for Marriage and Becoming Soul Mates for Life* (Wheaton, Ill.: Tyndale, 1995), 73.

2. Ibid.

3. Thomas Moore, *Soul Mates* (New York: HarperCollins, 1994), 237.

4. Ibid., 234.

5. Allender and Longman, 345.

6. Ibid., 44.

SOURCES CITED

Dan Allender and Tremper Longman, *Intimate Allies: Rediscovering God's Design for Marriage and Becoming Soul Mates for Life* (Tyndale, 1995).

Leslie Baxter and Barbara Montgomery, *Relating: Dialogues and Dialectics* (Guilford, 1996).

Gary Chapman, *The Five Love Languages: The Secret to Love That Lasts* (Northfield, 2010).

Andrew Christensen and Neil Jacobson, *Reconcilable Differences* (Guilford, 2000).

Rebecca Cutter, *When Opposites Attract: Right Brain / Left Brain Relationships and How to Make Them Work* (Dutton, 1994).

Elisabeth Dodds, *Marriage to a Difficult Man: The Uncommon Union of Jonathan and Sarah Edwards* (Westminster John Knox Press, 1971).

Sybil Evans and Sherry Cohen, *Hot Buttons: How to Resolve Conflict and Cool Everyone Down* (Cliff Street Books, 2000).

Ken Gire, *Windows of the Soul* (Zondervan, 1996).

John Gottman and Nan Silver, *The Seven Principles for Making Marriage Work* (Three Rivers Press, 1999).

John Gottman, *Why Marriages Succeed or Fail ... and How You Can Make Yours Last* (Fireside, 1994).

Eric Hoffer, *The Passionate State of Mind* (Buccaneer Books, 1955).

Eric Hoffer, *Reflections on the Human Condition* (HarperCollins, 1973).

David Keirsey and Marilyn Bates, *Please Understand Me: Character and Temperament Types* (Prometheus Nemesis, 1984).

Christine Leefeldt and Ernest Callenbach, *The Art of Friendship* (Berkley, 1981).

Charles Lickson, *Ironing It Out: Seven Simple Steps to Resolving Conflict* (Crisp Publications, 1996).

Thomas Moore, *Soul Mates* (HarperCollins, 1994).

Clifford Notarius and Howard Markman, *We Can Work It Out: How to Solve Conflicts, Save Your Marriage, and Strengthen Your Love for Each Other* (Penguin Putnam, 1993).

Susan Page, *How One of You Can Bring the Two of You Together: Breakthrough Strategies to Resolve Your Conflicts and Reignite Your Love* (Broadway Books, 1997).

Sally Springer and Georg Deutsch, *Left Brain / Right Brain,* 4th ed. (W. H. Freeman, 1993).

Scott Stanley, Daniel Trathen, Savanna McCain, and Milt Bryan, *A Lasting Promise: A Christian Guide to Fighting for Your Marriage* (Jossey-Bass, 1998).

Deborah Tannen, *You Just Don't Understand: Women and Men in Conversation* (Ballantine, 1990).

William Ury, *Getting to Peace: Transforming Conflict at Home, at Work, and in the World* (Viking, 1999).

James Walker, *Husbands Who Won't Lead and Wives Who Won't Follow* (Bethany, 1989).

Dudley Weeks, *The Eight Essential Steps to Conflict Resolution: Preserving Relationships at Work, at Home, and in the Community* (Putnam, 1994).

Michele Weiner-Davis, *Divorce Busting: A Step-by-Step Approach to Making Your Marriage Loving Again* (Simon & Schuster, 1992).

Women of Faith, ed., *Bring Home the Joy* (Zondervan, 1998).

Julia Wood, *Interpersonal Communication: Everyday Encounters,* 2d ed. (Wadsworth, 1999).

RECOMMENDED RESOURCES

WEBSITES

FamilyLife: http://familylife.com

Dr. Gary Chapman: www.garychapman.org/; www.5lovelanguages.com

Drs. Les & Leslie Parrott: www.realrelationships.com/

Gary Smalley: http://gosmalley.com/

BOOKS

For information on Tim Downs's novels, please visit http://timdowns.net.

Dr. Dan Allender and Tremper Longman, *Bold Love* (NavPress).

Dr. Dan B. Allender and Tremper Longman, *Intimate Allies* (Tyndale).

Dr. Gary Chapman, *The Five Love Languages: The Secret to Love That Lasts* (Northfield).

Gary Chapman and Jennifer Thomas, *The Five Love Languages of Apology: How to Experience Healing in All Your Relationships* (Northfield).

Tim and Joy Downs, *Fight Fair! Winning at Conflict Without Losing at Love* (Moody).

Emerson Eggerichs, *Love & Respect: The Love She Most Desires; the Respect He Desperately Needs* (Integrity).

Shaunti Feldhahn, *For Women Only: What You Need to Know About the Inner Lives of Men* (Multnomah).

Shaunti Feldhahn, *For Men Only: A Straightforward Guide to the Inner Lives of Women* (Multnomah).

Nancy Sebastian Meyer, *Talk Easy, Listen Hard: Real Communication for Two Really Different People* (Moody).

Drs. Les and Leslie Parrott, *The Complete Guide to Marriage Mentoring* (Zondervan).

Drs. Les and Leslie Parrott, *Trading Places: The Best Move You'll Ever Make in Marriage* (Zondervan).

Dennis and Barbara Rainey, *Staying Close: Stopping the Natural Drift Toward Isolation in Marriage* (Thomas Nelson).

Ken Sande and Tom Raabe, *Peacemaking for Families: A Biblical Guide to Managing Conflict in Your Home* (Tyndale).

Mitch Temple, *The Marriage Turnaround* (Moody).

Gary Thomas, *Sacred Influence: How God Uses Wives to Shape the Souls of Their Husbands* (Zondervan).

Gary Thomas, *Sacred Marriage: What if God Designed Marriage to Make Us Holy More than to Make Us Happy?* (Zondervan).

Dr. H. Norman Wright, *Communication: Key to Your Marriage* (Regal).

ACKNOWLEDGMENTS

Thanks to our dear friends and family who prayed for us and shared the stories of their own marriages: Tom and Linda Barrett, Mark and Julie Bontrager, Dan and Julie Brenton, Ben and Janet Burns, Bill and Laura Burns, Bobby and Ann Clampett, Doug and Patty Daily, Mark and Erin Donalson, Steve and Myra Ellis, Jon and Noonie Fugler, Doug and Terri Haigh, Bill and Rese Hood, Jim and Renee Keller, Kent and Kim Kramer, Glenn and Beth Melhorn, Al and Diane Meyer, Tim and Noreen Muehlhoff, Mike and Renee Seay, Dave and Sande Sunde, Sam and Carol Thomsen, J. T. and Enid Walker, and John and Susan Yates. We appreciate all of your labor on our behalf and the encouragement that fueled our writing!

Thanks to our good friend Tim Muehlhoff for reading our manuscript as it progressed and offering a critical eye.

Thanks to our editor, Cheryl Dunlop, for her insights, corrections, and contributions to the original text, and thanks to Pam Pugh who helped us with revising and updating the current edition.

Thanks to our agent, Lee Hough, for his sound guidance, wise counsel, and constant encouragement.

And a special thanks to the hundreds of couples who shared their struggles with us at FamilyLife's Weekend to Remember Conferences. We hope this book gives something back to each of you.

FIGHT FAIR!

WINNING AT CONFLICT WITHOUT LOSING AT LOVE

ISBN-13: 978-0-8024-1428-1

When couples fight, tempers flare, tongues loosen, and behavior occurs that can cause major damage to the relationship. Tim and Joy Downs have written *Fight Fair!* to teach couples how to have healthy disagreements. It is a "rule book" for married couples to ensure that their conflict is God-honoring and respectful of their partner. Readers will find this book full of helpful, very practical tips they can immediately apply to ensure that future conflicts don't create permanent scars.

MOODY
PUBLISHERS

www.MoodyPublishers.com